Christ,
Our New Covenant
Prophet, Priest and King

John G. Reisinger

D0840453

Books by
John G. Reisinger

Abraham's Four Seeds

The Believer's Sabbath

But I Say Unto You

Chosen in Eternity

Christ, Lord and Lawgiver Over the Church

Continuity and Discontinuity

Grace

The Grace of Our Sovereign God

In Defense of Jesus, the New Lawgiver

John Bunyan on the Sabbath

Limited Atonement

The New Covenant Church – Ekklesia – of Christ

The New Birth

New Covenant Theology and Prophecy

Our Sovereign God

Perseverance of the Saints

Studies in Galatians

Studies in Ecclesiastes

Tablets of Stone

The Sovereignty of God and Prayer

The Sovereignty of God in Providence

Total Depravity

What is the Christian Faith?

When Should a Christian Leave a Church?

Christ,
Our New Covenant
Prophet, Priest and King

John G. Reisinger

5317 Wye Creek Drive, Frederick, MD 21703-6938
301-473-8781 | info@newcovenantmedia.com
www.NewCovenantMedia.com

Christ, Our New Covenant Prophet, Priest and King

ISBN 13: 978-1-928965-63-3

Dedication

This book is dedicated to the Colin Wellum family of Burlington, Ontario. Dr. Wellum, his wife and four sons are a godly family in the full meaning of that biblical word. It has been my privilege to know them for many years. They have all exhibited the characteristics of true godliness.

Table of Contents

Introduction

The Old Testament Scriptures set forth Moses, Aaron (and Melchizedek)[1] and David as types of Christ in his work as Prophet, Priest and King. In each case, the New Testament Scriptures demonstrate exactly how Christ fulfills all three of these offices.

One, Christ is "that Prophet" who fulfills the promise God made to Moses in Deuteronomy 18:15: "The Lord your God will raise up for you a prophet like me from among your own brothers. You must listen to him."

Two, Christ is the "Priest in the order of Melchizedek" as promised in Psalm 110:4: "The LORD has sworn and will not change his mind: 'You are a priest forever, in the order of Melchizedek.'" Christ is also the high priest who replaces Aaron and the Levitical priesthood.

Three, Christ is David's greater Son who established the everlasting kingdom promised to David and now sits on the throne in fulfillment of the Davidic covenant made in 2 Samuel 7:12, 13: "When your days are over and you rest with your fathers, I will raise up your offspring to succeed you, who will come from your own body, and I will establish his kingdom. He is the one who will build a house for my Name, and I will establish the throne of his kingdom forever."

Commentators and preachers of all persuasions have set forth these truths concerning the three offices of Christ. The *Westminster Larger Catechism* is typical.

Question 42: Why was our Mediator called Christ?

---

[1] Both Aaron and Melchizedek are types of Christ. We will note the essential difference between the two later when we consider Christ as our Priest.

Answer: Our Mediator was called Christ, because he was anointed with the Holy Ghost above measure; and so set apart, and fully furnished with all authority and ability, to execute the offices of prophet, priest, and king of his church, in the estate both of his humiliation and exaltation.

Question 43: How does Christ execute the office of a prophet?

Answer: Christ executes the office of a prophet, in his revealing to the church, in all ages, by his Spirit and Word, in divers ways of administration, the whole will of God, in all things concerning their edification and salvation.

Question 44: How does Christ execute the office of a priest?

Answer: Christ executes the office of a priest, in his once offering himself a sacrifice without spot to God, to be a reconciliation for the sins of his people; and in making continual intercession for them.

Question 45: How does Christ execute the office of a king?

Answer: Christ executes the office of a king, in calling out of the world a people to himself, and giving them officers, laws, and censures, by which he visibly governs them; in bestowing saving grace upon his elect, rewarding their obedience, and correcting them for their sins, preserving and supporting them under all their temptations and sufferings, restraining and overcoming all their enemies, and powerfully ordering all things for his own glory, and their good; and also in taking vengeance on the rest, who know not God, and obey not the gospel.

The New Testament Scriptures clearly show that: 1) Christ is the true and final Prophet who replaces Moses; 2) Christ is the true and successful Priest who replaces the Aaronic priesthood; 3) Christ is the true and everlasting King who fulfills the covenant promise to David. We will look at the passages setting forth these truths.

The men who held these three offices under the old covenant controlled, in one way or another, the entire life, worship and morality of the theocratic nation of Israel, the old covenant people of God. Christ, as the new covenant Prophet, Priest and King, controls the entire life, worship and morality of the church, the new covenant people of God.

The Holy Spirit, in the New Testament Scriptures, used powerful object lessons to show, in each case, how Christ is the fulfillment of all three of these types.

1) *The Mount of Transfiguration* (Matt. 17:1-6) is the object lesson that shows the new Prophet has replaced Moses as prophet and lawgiver. The new Prophet also replaced all of the old covenant prophets as God's spokespersons. The message from heaven saying, "Listen to my Son" is the Father showing the change from the old authority to the new and final authority. This is the same message proclaimed in the book of Hebrews (Heb. 1:1-3). Christ is the last and final prophet. He has given us the full and final message of God. God has said all he has to say in his Son.

2) *The rending of the veil of the Temple* from top to bottom at the moment of Christ's death (Matt. 27:50-51) is the object lesson showing that the new Priest has replaced Aaron and fulfilled the Melchizedek prophecy. Again, this message is explicit in Hebrews (Heb. 9:1-10; 10:19-22). The message that we may now come boldly to the throne of grace by the new and living way now opened through Christ's work on the cross (Heb. 10:19, 20) could never have been preached as long as the Levitical priesthood was in effect, and the veil in the temple was hanging in place.

3) *The gift of tongues on the Day of Pentecost* (Acts 2:1-36) is the object lesson showing that the resurrection and ascension of Christ to sit on the throne of David has established the kingdom promised to David and prophesied in both Joel 2 and 2 Samuel 7. The message is "bow in repentance, faith and

assurance before the newly crowned Lord" (Philip. 2:9-11), or as the Psalmist said, "Kiss the Son" (Psalm 2:12).

Dispensationalism clearly sees the ministry of Moses as prophet and Aaron as priest as clear pictures foreshadowing the work of Christ in behalf of the church. Some of the most heartwarming and Christ exalting teaching that I have ever heard or read was from the ministry of men from the Brethren Assemblies preaching on the typology of the Tabernacle. They rightly saw Christ's work as Priest on behalf of the church in everything. However, when they came to the prophets all they could see was Israel and an earthly millennium. Christ's present Kingship over the church was not to be found in any of the Prophets. The church was a hidden mystery until first revealed to Paul and set forth in Ephesians. The message of the prophets only involved a future earthly and Jewish millennium. In this theology, Christ is Prophet and Priest over the church but not a present King over the church. He is only a *coming* King over a future redeemed Israel and not a present King over a present redeemed church made up of both saved Jews and Gentiles. Some of my dispensational brethren insist that Christ is "Lord over the church and King over Israel." His kingly rule was postponed until a future date.

Covenant Theologians see Christ as David's son already established on David's throne in heaven. He is presently King just as much as he is Prophet and Priest. They also have no trouble seeing Aaron being replaced as High Priest by the Lord Jesus. However, they will not allow Christ to be a Lawgiver who replaces Moses as lawgiver. They will acknowledge Christ is the Prophet promised in Deuteronomy 18:15 but insist his prophetic work was to merely give the true interpretation of the Law that God gave to Moses. Our Lord does not change in any way any moral law given by Moses nor does he add any new laws to those given through Moses.

In other words, our Lord is the last and greatest exegete, or interpreter, of the Law given to Moses, but he is only an interpreter, he is not a lawgiver in his own right. He gives no new moral laws or in any way changes those laws Moses taught. Christ is the last and greatest exegete of Moses, but Moses is the full and final lawgiver! Christ does not replace Moses as lawgiver in the same sense that he replaces Aaron as priest. We will expand on this when we cover Christ as Prophet.[2]

In Covenant Theology, the so-called "moral law,"[3] meaning the Ten Commandments, cannot be changed in any way, even by the Son of God himself. Moses' ministry as lawgiver over the conscience is just as much in effect for a Christian today as it was for an Israelite under the old covenant. Those who hold this theology would never think of sending a believer back under the old covenant to have Aaron offer a lamb for them, and yet those same people insist that we must send believers back to Moses to learn morality and ethics. We must treat Moses as the full and final lawgiver and Christ as merely the true interpreter of Moses. It is our belief that Christ fulfills all three offices, Prophet, Priest and King in this dispensation and in the church. We believe Christ replaces Moses as Lawgiver in exactly the same sense that he replaces Aaron as Priest. We also believe that Christ is presently seated on David's promised throne as King of Kings and Lord of Lords.

---

[2] For a detailed defense of this position, see *In Defense of the Decalogue,* by Dr. Richard Barcellos. For a detailed criticism of Barcellos' book, see my *In Defense of Jesus, the New Lawgiver.*

[3] I use the words *so-called* because nowhere does Scripture teach the law can be divided into three codes of law. There are laws that are civil, laws that are moral and laws that are ceremonial but there are not three codes of law where two are done away with in Christ and one, the moral, is retained with no changes.

Several things are essential in this discussion in helping us with the knotty question of "continuity/discontinuity." The ministries of all three offices, prophet, priest and king, were tied up with the old covenant. Moses was the mediator of the old covenant that established Israel as the special nation of God's uniquely chosen people. Aaron was the high priest who administrated the whole system of sacrificial offerings. David was the king given the special kingdom prophecy that one of his sons would sit on his throne in an eternal kingdom. The New Testament Scriptures showing the fulfillment of the three offices prophesied in Old Testament Scriptures clearly demonstrate the failure and end of the old covenant and all it brought into being. A totally new covenant has fulfilled the promises of the old covenant and completely replaced it. The church has a new Prophet, a new Priest, and a new King.

This truth is set forth in a much misunderstood text.

> *Therefore if any man be in Christ, he is a new creature: old things are passed away; behold all things have become new* (2 Cor. 5:17 KJV).

The NIV is a far better translation.

> *Therefore, if anyone is in Christ, he is a new creation; the old has gone, the new has come!*[4] (2 Cor. 5:17).

Paul is not saying, "If a person becomes a Christian, his whole life is changed. His old sinful habits are all gone and he lives a totally different life." It is certainly true that biblical conversion radically changes the life style of the person converted. This truth is a major theme of the New Testament Scriptures. However, that is not Paul's point in this text. Paul is not dealing with sanctification in this text; he is dealing with the new creation brought in by Christ through the new covenant. The contrast is not with how radically different lost

---

[4] A.W. Pink has an excellent treatment of this text in a booklet called *Pink Jewels* (MacDill AFB, FL: Tyndale Bible Society, n.d.) 7 ff.

and saved people live, but with describing a person being under the new covenant as opposed to being under the old covenant.

The apostle is contrasting the old Adam creation with the new Christ creation. Both the old things that have passed away, and the new things that have become new in this text are in aorist tense. That means that the old things spoken of have all, with no exceptions, "once for all" passed away in totality. Likewise, the things that have become new mean "all things" without exception have become, "once and for all," totally new. If this is describing the change in a Christian's life, then Christians are sinless and totally holy. Who among us can say that every single bad thing in their life has forever gone away and everything, without a single exception, has become totally new, different and permanent? This text is not talking about sanctification but justification. It is not describing our day to day state but our eternal standing before God in Christ. Every Christian can say, "Many, even possibly 'most,' things are in the *process* of becoming new," but no Christian can say, "all things without exception have once and for all become new." That would be tantamount to saying, "I have become a sinless, perfect person."

The book of Hebrews is the commentary on 2 Corinthians 5:17. If a man is "in Christ," he has been crucified with Christ, dead, buried and raised with Christ, and at this very moment is seated in heavenly places in Christ Jesus. He is part of two different creations at the same time. He is part of a physical creation and also part of a spiritual creation. To be "in Christ" is to be a part of the "new creation," or the "new man" mentioned in Ephesians 2:15. The new creation is the church viewed as the body of Christ that was created on the day of Pentecost. To be "in Christ" is to be under grace and baptized into the body of Christ. It is to be under the new covenant or in the new creation. In the new creation, everything is totally, radically and permanently new. John MacArthur has stated it clearly:

> BETTER EVERYTHING:
>
> In this epistle [Hebrews], contrasts reigns. Everything presented is presented as better: a better hope, a better testament, a better promise, a better sacrifice, a better substance, a better country, a better resurrection, a better everything. Jesus Christ is presented here as the supreme Best. And we are presented as being in him and as dwelling in a completely new dimension—the heavenlies. We read of the heavenly Christ, the heavenly calling, the heavenly gift, the heavenly country, the heavenly Jerusalem, and our names being written in the heavenlies. Everything is new. Everything is better. We don't need the old.[5]

It is not recorded in Scripture but the Jews may well have taunted the early Christians on several fronts. The first one would have gone something like this: "You guys cannot have a true religion since you do not have any of the things essential to a religion. You have no prophet, no priest, no temple, no sacrifice, no covenant or any of the things that are an essential part of a religion." The writer to the book of Hebrews answers such a taunt by stressing that the Christian has everything the Jews have, and in every instance what the Christian has is something better. The church has a better prophet, a better priest, a better temple, a better sacrifice, a better covenant, etc. All things are not only totally new under the new covenant, they are also better than anything under the old covenant. The old is totally fulfilled and has vanished away. The new has come and established everything new and complete.

There are two very important principles established in a correct understanding of 2 Corinthians 5:17 and the book of

---

[5] John MacArthur, *The MacArthur New Testament Commentary, Hebrews* (Chicago: Moody Press, 1983) xix.

Hebrews. First, everything in the old covenant has been fulfilled and has permanently passed away. Everything in the new covenant is radically, totally new and nothing will pass away except faith will give way to sight. However, even though everything under the new covenant is new, all of these new things were prophesied in the Old Testament Scriptures as future realities to come in Messiah's reign. As we will see when we develop the truth of Prophet, Priest and King, the new merely fulfills what was promised in the old. Our Lord fulfills the expectations that grew out of the promises that God gave in the Old Testament Scriptures. In one sense, the new makes no sense without the old and in another sense the old is not even close to complete without the new. Many people quote Augustine's famous statement, "The new is in the old concealed and the old is in the new revealed," but they really don't consistently carry that through in detail. They either read the New Testament back into the Old Testament and try to Christianize Judaism, or they read the Old Testament into the New Testament and try to Judaize Christianity.

The question of continuity/discontinuity is not the primary subject of this book. However, it should be clear that the subject does directly impinge on the relationship of the old and new covenants. Understanding how much better Christ's ministry of Prophet, Priest and King is when compared with Moses, Aaron and David clearly involves continuity and discontinuity. Aaron and David's ministries are clear examples of discontinuity expressed in terms of promise and fulfillment. It is essential that the comparison of the old and new covenants, especially in the book of Hebrews, be seen as a comparison of Judaism and Christianity and not baby versus mature Christians. Again, John MacArthur has said it far better than we could. By the way, MacArthur's commentary on Hebrews is one of the best treatments of Hebrews in print.

The Contrast between Christianity and Judaism.

Throughout the book of Hebrews, the many comparisons and contrasts are basically between Christianity and Judaism. This truth is essential to a proper interpretation of the epistle.

The central theme and message of the book of Hebrews is the superiority of the New Covenant to the Old, that is, of Christianity to Judaism. Within this theme are the sub themes of the superiority of the new priesthood to the old, the new sacrifice to the old ones, the new Mediator to the old ones, and so on. This is the key that unlocks every section of Hebrews, and to use any other key is, I believe, to make forced entry.

In the book of Hebrews the Holy Spirit is not contrasting two kinds of Christianity. He is not contrasting immature Christians and mature ones. He is contrasting Judaism and Christianity …. He is contrasting the substance and the shadow, the pattern and the reality, the visible and the invisible, the facsimile and the real thing, the type and the anti-type, the picture and the actual.

The Old Testament essentially is God's revelation of pictures and types, which are fulfilled in Christ in the New Testament. The book of Hebrews, therefore, compares and contrasts the two parts of God's revelation that our division of the Bible reflects.[6]

We will see this contrast as we compare the ministry of Moses, Aaron and David with the ministry of our Lord Jesus Christ. We will see three great and godly men who, despite their faithfulness and godliness, nonetheless had to be replaced. None of them, or all of them put together, could accomplish the goal of God's sovereign grace. That great work took a new Prophet, a new Priest and a new King. A fellow pastor, Chad Bresson, wrote the following:

---

[6] Ibid., 127, 128

One way in which this *telos* has been achieved in the fullness of the gospel is the way in which Jesus fulfills all the mediatorial offices of Messiah: He is more than just the Prophet, Priest and King of his people: He is the Prophet and the *message*; Priest and the *sacrifice*; King and the *law*. All things, indeed, have joined in him. He is the perfection of God's purpose.

The New Testament sets forth Christ as the true and final Prophet. God has said all that he has to say in his Son, see Hebrews 1:1-3. He is the new covenant Prophet.

> *For Moses said, 'The Lord your God will raise up for you a prophet like me from among your own people; you must listen to everything he tells you. Anyone who does not listen to him will be completely cut off from among his people.'*

> *"Indeed, all the prophets from Samuel on, as many as have spoken, have foretold these days. And you are heirs of the prophets and of the covenant God made with your fathers. He said to Abraham, 'Through your offspring all peoples on earth will be blessed.' When God raised up his servant, he sent him first to you to bless you by turning each of you from your wicked ways"* (Acts 3:22-26).

The New Testament sets forth Christ as the very kind of priest that sinners need to adequately represent them before God. He can bring all for whom he died into the presence of God fully justified.

> *Now there have been many of those priests, since death prevented them from continuing in office; but because Jesus lives forever, he has a permanent priesthood. Therefore he is able to save completely those who come to God through him, because he lives to intercede for them.*

> *Such a high priest meets our need—one who is holy, blameless, pure, set apart from sinners, exalted above the heavens. Unlike the other high priests, he does not need to offer sacrifices day after day, first for his own sins, and then for the sins of the people. He sacrificed for their sins once for all when he offered himself* (Heb. 7:23–27).

The New Testament sets forth Christ as King. He not only rules as King, he guards and protects all his subjects. "… the government will be on his shoulders" (Isa. 9:6).

They will make war against the Lamb, but the Lamb will overcome them because he is Lord of lords and King of kings … (Rev. 17:14).

Christ,
Our New Covenant Lawgiver
Chapter 1

Christ is "that Prophet" who fulfills the prophecy concerning the new lawgiver who would replace Moses. The Old Testament prophecy is recorded in Deuteronomy 18:15-19, and the object lesson demonstrating that the prophecy has been fulfilled is the Mount of Transfiguration (Matt. 17:1-6; Mark 9:2-8; Luke 9:28-36). Scripture makes it clear that the Jews not only knew about the promise that God made to Moses concerning a new prophet; they were looking forward to its fulfillment. They asked John the Baptist,

> They asked him, "Then who are you? Are you Elijah?"
>
> He said, "I am not."
>
> "Are you the Prophet?"
>
> He answered, "No." (John 1:21).

Their point of reference was Deuteronomy 18.

A bit later, John again mentions the expectation of the promised prophet. After Jesus had fed five thousand people with two small fish and five small barley loaves, he told them to gather up the leftovers.

> So they gathered them and filled twelve baskets with the pieces of the five barley loaves left over by those who had eaten.
>
> After the people saw the miraculous sign that Jesus did, they began to say, "Surely this is the Prophet who is to come into the world" (John 6:13-14).

Again, their expectation came from Deuteronomy 18. This is a very important section of Scripture. Let us examine it carefully and see exactly what God was promising. Notice that the new Prophet will speak with the full authority of God himself. I have added bold numbers within the passage to mark four significant points.

> (1) *I will raise up for them a prophet like you from among their brothers; (2) I will put my words in his mouth, and (3) he will tell them everything I command him. If anyone does not listen to (4) my words that the prophet speaks in my name, I myself will call him to account* (Deut. 18:18-19).

Point One: Exactly how is Jesus "like Moses"? The two primary likenesses of Moses and Jesus are that (1) they are both mediators of a specific covenant, and (2) they are both lawgivers. They both mediated covenants that established nations. Moses meditated the covenant that established God's earthly people, the nation of Israel, and Jesus is the Mediator of the new covenant that established the church, the true Israel of God. Both Moses and Christ gave the specific laws under which the covenant people of God to whom they minister are to live and by which they will be judged. Moses is the mediator and lawgiver of the old covenant and Christ is the Mediator and Lawgiver of the new covenant. Moses is the lawgiver for Israel; the chosen earthly nation of God living under the old covenant. Christ is the Lawgiver for the true people of God living under the new covenant. Additionally, God promises that the new prophet will be "from among their brethren." The author of the letter to the Hebrews stresses the humanity of Jesus Christ (Heb. 2:11-18; 10:5-10). Jesus Christ fulfills this part of the prophecy on both details; he is "like Moses" as a lawgiver. He is also "like Moses" in that he is both a human being and a seed of Abraham.

Point Two: All true prophets speak the words of God when they prophesy, but at other times, they speak their own words. There is no question that Moses was the greatest of all prophets until the advent of our Lord. Moses is the only prophet that ever spoke face-to-face with God, but not every word that Moses spoke during his ministry was directly from God. The words of Moses spoken merely as a man were no more inspired than the words you and I speak today. Jesus did not have a one-time face-to-face encounter with God; he came from an eternal existence with the Father. John records Jesus' explanation of which he spoke:

> ...I am [the one I claim to be] and that I do nothing on my own but speak just what the Father has taught me (John 8:28).

> For I did not speak of my own accord, but the Father who sent me commanded me what to say and how to say it. I know that his command leads to eternal life. So whatever I say is just what the Father has told me to say" (John 12:49-50).

> ... These words you hear are not my own; they belong to the Father who sent me" (John 14:24).

It is exegetically impossible to attempt to make these words mean that Jesus came, not to give any new revelation or laws about morality and holiness, but he came only to give us the true meaning and interpretation of the highest laws that were already given through Moses at Mount Sinai. Moses, despite his greatness above all the prophets, must still speak only as a prophet. Our Lord not only speaks as a prophet, he speaks as the Creator; he speaks as God himself.

Point Three: According to Hebrews 1:1-3, our Lord is the full and final revelation of God. In his Son, God has said all that he has to say. Not only does Christ bring God's full and final message, Christ himself actually is *the Message* as well as the *Messenger*. Moses spoke as a faithful servant in God's house; Jesus spoke as the Son who built God's house and who is in charge of that house.

> Therefore, holy brothers, who share in the heavenly calling, fix your thoughts on Jesus, the apostle and high priest whom we confess. He was faithful to the one who appointed him, just as Moses was faithful in all God's house. Jesus has been found worthy of greater honor than Moses, just as the builder of a house has greater honor

than the house itself. For every house is built by someone, but God is the builder of everything. Moses was faithful as a servant in all God's house, testifying to what would be said in the future. But Christ is faithful as a son over God's house. And we are his house, if we hold on to our courage and the hope of which we boast (Heb. 3:1-6).

Point Four: The new Lawgiver gives some new and higher house rules that are more appropriate for the new spiritual house. As mentioned above, Moses alone of all the prophets spoke face-to-face with God, but even he, like all other prophets, had to preface his speech with, "Thus saith the Lord" when he repeated a specific message that God had given to him. Only our Lord could say, "But I say unto you" and speak with the authority of God himself. Moses, like all true prophets, could claim that "God told me to say this," but only Jesus could say, "I am speaking as God. I am speaking with the full authority of God himself. I am telling you that you must believe what I say *just because I said it!*" In Deuteronomy 18, God promises that he will judge men based on an individual's attitude to the words of the new prophet, and Jesus repeats that idea.

"There is a judge for the one who rejects me and does not accept my words; that very word which I spoke will condemn him at the last day" (John 12:48).

These words cannot be tortured to mean, "There is a judge for the one who refuses to accept my true interpretation of Moses."

Ironically, this unique authority of Jesus Christ as the new Lawgiver is at the heart of a great controversy in Reformed, especially Reformed Baptist, circles today. I have been the subject of several books and quite a few articles that claim I am an "antinomian" simply because I believe that Christ is a new lawgiver who replaces Moses. My great sin is believing that the Ten Commandments were indeed the highest law and revelation of the character of God ever given up to that point in time, but our Lord gives his church an even higher standard. I believe Jesus not only gives his church a much fuller revelation of God's holy character, he also gives the new covenant people of God a higher moral standard. The holiness demanded of a new covenant believer indwelt by the Holy Spirit is greater than that required under the law. One preacher who disagreed with me on this point insisted, "Christ is a Law-keeper not a Law-giver." I replied, "I believe he is both." I believe that Christ, in the "But I say unto you" contrasts in the Sermon on the Mount, is clearly establishing himself as a new Lawgiver in contrast to Moses as the old lawgiver. In the Sermon on the Mount, Christ gives us higher and more spiritual laws than Moses gave, or could have given, to Israel under a covenant of law.[7]

We insist as loudly as we can that Christ never once *contradicts* Moses. *Contrasting* two things to emphasize their difference and show why one is better than the other one is not at all the same as saying they contradict each other. If anyone ever teaches that Christ contradicted Moses or says Moses said something that was wrong, they are clearly destroying the unity of the Scriptures. Our Lord never says, or in any way implies, that Moses was wrong. He does contrast his teaching with that of Moses and clearly claims the law of his kingdom of grace is a higher law than that given to Moses for Israel.

When Hebrews insists that there is a new and better covenant, the writer is not saying the old covenant was either bad or wrong. He is merely insisting that the new covenant is much better than the old covenant. If that were not true, there never would have been a need for a new covenant as a replacement. Christ is contrasting a theocratic earthly kingdom based on "good, holy, and just" law with a spiritual kingdom

---

[7] For a detailed proof of this assertion, see my *But I Say unto You* (Frederick, MD: New Covenant Media, 2006)

based on pure grace and higher laws. Both kingdoms, though different, are righteous and good and both come from God. However, one is *better* than the other one. Actually, one prepares the way for the second one. Christ is contrasting the essence of the very nature of law and grace, but he in no way is denying that both law and grace are holy, righteous and good. Our Lord is contrasting the theocratic kingdom established under Moses based on pure law with his newly founded kingdom based on pure grace. The latter is far superior to the former, but in no sense was the former wrong or bad.

Living under the covenant of law given through Moses and living under the gracious covenant of grace established by Christ are two different things. No one questions that the laws God gave to Moses to govern the nation of Israel are "holy, righteous and good" (Rom. 7:12). Those laws fulfill God's primary intention to convict a rebellious nation of its guilt and push them to believe the gospel promised to Abraham. Those same laws are not high enough to govern saints of God indwelt by the Holy Spirit. This is what our Lord is stating in Matthew 19:8, 9. He specifically insists that the true nature of most Israelites, even though they were "redeemed by (animal) blood" was that of hard-hearted sinners. Jesus told the Pharisees, "Moses, because of the hardness of your hearts, permitted you to divorce your wives, but from the beginning it was not so" (NKJV). Hard-hearted sinners need a covenant of law to convict them of sin. God's true church, living under the new covenant, does not have any hard hearted-sinners. They have been given new hearts that love righteousness. They have hearts upon which God's law has been written. They are all regenerated. They all "know the Lord" in saving faith (Heb. 8:11).

God provided Israel with the Mosaic laws concerning easy divorce and polygamy only because Israel's "hearts were hard" (Matt. 19:1-9). I repeat: none of God's new covenant people have a hard heart. They all have new hearts that yearn to please God. The laws that God gave to hard-hearted sinners under the old covenant in order to convict those sinners of their need of grace are not of the same nature as the laws given to regenerate saints with new hearts under the new covenant. The laws, or rules, that govern a child of God living under grace will always make higher demands than the law or rules that govern hard-hearted sinners living under a covenant of law.[8] I have a real problem trying to understand why this is so difficult for some people to grasp when Scripture is so clear.

A "catch question" that enables a certain brand of theologian to immediately label you as either orthodox or antinomian is this: "Do you believe the Ten Commandments are the rule of life for a Christian today?" Anything but an unqualified yes earns you the label of *antinomian*. My response to that question is: "I believe the Ten Commandments, not as they were written on stone and given to Israel as covenant terms,[9]

---

[8] Both dispensationalism and Covenant Theology forget that Israel, as a nation, was the *earthly* "loved, chosen, redeemed, called" people of God even though most of those "loved, chosen, redeemed, called" people were ungodly rebels who died in unbelief and went to hell (Heb. 3:16-19). We dare not attach, as both dispensationalism and Covenant Theology do, new covenant spiritual meanings to the redemptive words Scripture uses of Israel as a physical nation. This is a root error of both dispensationalism and Covenant Theology.

[9] Very few writers or theologians acknowledge the fact that the Ten Commandments constituted the basic covenant document, or the summary document of the old covenant. Their theology insists that the Ten Commandments must be trans-covenantal. However, Scripture makes it clear in specific texts that the author of those texts considered the Ten Commandments written on stone as the "terms of the covenant" God made with Israel at Sinai. Exodus 34:27-29: *Then the LORD said to Moses, "Write down these words, for in accordance with these*

but as they are *clearly interpreted and applied by our Lord and his apostles in the new covenant Scriptures,* are a very real *part* of a Christian's rule of life today." [10] The Ten Commandments *contain* moral law, but the Ten Commandments are not THE moral law. Strangely enough some of the people who get the most upset when we make those statements will say the very same thing using different words.

Dr. Richard Barcellos has written extensively against what I believe concerning New Covenant Theology. He wrote a book titled *In Defense of the Decalogue.* [11] The major thesis of his book is exactly what the title states. He is defending his belief that the Ten Commandments, as written on the tablets of the covenant (Ex. 34:27, 28), are the unchanging moral law of God. He rejects our contention that Jesus is the new Lawgiver

---

*words I have **made a covenant** with you and with Israel." Moses was there with the LORD forty days and forty nights without eating bread or drinking water. And he wrote on the tablets **the words of the covenant—the Ten Commandments.** When Moses came down from Mount Sinai with the **two tablets of the Testimony** in his hands, he was not aware that his face was radiant because he had spoken with the LORD. Deuteronomy 4:13: He declared to you **his covenant, the Ten Commandments,** which he commanded you to follow and then **wrote them on two stone tablets**. Deuteronomy 9:9-11: When I went up on the mountain to receive **the tablets of stone, the tablets of the covenant** that the LORD had made with you, I stayed on the mountain forty days and forty nights; I ate no bread and drank no water. The LORD gave me **two stone tablets inscribed by the finger of God. On them were all the commandments the** LORD **proclaimed to you on the mountain out of the fire,** on the day of the assembly. At the end of the forty days and forty nights, the LORD gave me the **two stone tablets, the tablets of the covenant.**

[10] For a detailed study of the place of the Ten Commandments in the history of redemption, see my *Tablets of Stone* (Frederick, MD: New Covenant Media, 2004).

[11] We have written a lengthy response to Barcellos and laid out what we really believe. See my *In Defense of Jesus, the New Lawgiver* (Frederick, MD: New Covenant Media, 2008).

who replaces Moses in exactly the same manner that Jesus replaces Aaron. After Barcellos sets forth what he thinks we believe, he gives us his version of what he believes Matthew 5:17-20 really means.

> *What Jesus is saying is that the Old Testament is still binding upon His people,* but not in the same way it used to be. [12] (Italics in the original).

But that is precisely what we believe and teach! When we say the identical same thing but use some different words, Barcellos calls us "antinomians." When Barcellos makes that statement it is good theology, but when we state the same truth using different words, we are heretics. Barcellos then quotes New Testament scholar Vern Poythress.

> All the commandments of the law are binding on Christians …, but the way in which they are binding is determined by the authority of Christ and the fulfillment that takes place in His work." [13]

Again, we could not state what we believe any better or any more clearly than Poythress has done.

The entire Bible, all sixty-six books, interpreted through the lens of the new covenant, is the Christian's rule of life today. Is that not what both Barcellos and Poythress are saying? I am fully aware that nearly everyone says they believe we must interpret the Old Testament in the light of the New, but in reality both Covenant Theology and dispensationalism have their entire systems of theology in place before they get out of the book of Genesis. Some theologians say, "If you cannot find the seed and root of a doctrine in the first eleven chapters of Genesis it is not a biblical doctrine."

---

[12] Richard Barcellos, *In Defense of the Decalogue: A Critique of New Covenant Theology* (Enumclaw, WA: WinePress Publishing, 2001) 65.

[13] Ibid.

I could also respond to the earlier stated catch question by saying, "The Ten Commandments are far too low a standard for a child of God indwelt by the Holy Spirit and living under grace." We are not in any sense whatever anti-law. One of our major premises is that the clear objective laws that Christ has given to Christians are higher laws than God gave to Moses. I keep asking the people who accuse me of being an antinomian how it is possible for us to be "against law," which is the essence of antinomianism, when we vehemently insist that Christ gives us higher laws than Moses gave Israel. How can belief in higher law be twisted to mean against law? I have yet to receive an answer to this valid question. To label what we have stated as antinomian is ludicrous. We insist that Christ is a new lawgiver who replaces Moses exactly as it was prophesized in Deuteronomy 18. That is labeled as "heresy" only because it contradicts the third maxim of Covenant Theology, the "one unchanging moral code for all men in all ages." Covenant Theology will not allow even our Lord himself to change, or add anything to, one single law of Moses. Moses is king of the campus in the conscience of a believer in the system of Covenant Theology. In that system, Christ, in no sense, can replace Moses as a new Lawgiver. Christ merely gives us the true meaning of the law of Moses. [14]

---

[14] We must not confuse the "unity of the Scriptures" with the "unity of the covenants." We accept without question the "unity of the Scriptures." God has one unchanging sovereign purpose in grace (Eph. 1:1-14) but the old and new covenants are two distinctly different covenants. The Scriptures know nothing about the old and new covenants being different "administrations" or "versions" of one and the same covenant.

Christ, The Lawgiver Who Replaces Moses
Chapter 2

In the preceding chapter we started to talk about Christ, our new covenant Prophet, being a true Lawgiver who replaces Moses in exactly the same way that he replaces Aaron as High Priest. We have noted how important Deuteronomy 18:15-19 is in any discussion of Christ as Prophet. Let us look carefully at a new covenant text with references back to Deuteronomy 18:15-19. In John 17:8 our Lord is speaking to his Father.

> *For I have given to them the words which You have given Me; and they have received them, and have known surely that I came forth from You; and they have believed that You sent Me* (NKJV).

How can responsible exegesis make this statement mean that Jesus never gives any new law, but merely gives the true interpretation of what Moses has already spoken? Jesus does not say or imply that his work was merely to interpret Moses. He has manifested God's name to the elect (John 17:6) by speaking "the words the Father gave him." We cannot reduce such a statement to mean that the Father did no more than give his Son the true exegesis of the "eternal unchanging moral law of God" that he had given to Moses. The words in the prophecy of Deuteronomy 18:15-19 demand that a new Lawgiver[15] will come who will give new revelation. If Christ merely interprets Moses without giving any new laws, he simply does not fulfill this prophecy in Deuteronomy 18. You

---

[15] Genesis 49:10 clearly prophesies that Messiah will be the true Lawgiver in the lineage of Judah.

cannot make *"For I have given to them the words which You have given Me"* to mean "I have given them the correct meaning of the words you gave to Moses."

In order to understand why some theologians cannot allow Christ to be a new Lawgiver who replaces Moses as lawgiver in exactly the same way that he replaces Aaron as high priest, we must clearly understand the basic presuppositions of their system of theology. One very vital question helps to pinpoint those unstated warrants: With whom is Christ contrasting himself in the Sermon on the Mount when he says, "But I say unto you"? This is a key question. Is Christ here speaking merely as an exegete of Moses or is he speaking as a prophet and new lawgiver in his own right? In the context, it reads as though Christ is contrasting his teaching with that of Moses, but that exegesis is anathema to Covenant Theology. That system of theology insists Christ is not in any way contrasting his teaching with that of Moses. He is only refuting the false misunderstanding the Pharisees have of Moses.

We must be certain we understand what people actually believe before we can interact with them. Covenant Theology has three basic maxims upon which their theology of law rests. These maxims are not debatable.

ONE: There is one unchanging covenant of grace in all ages for all men (Westminster Confession of Faith 7:4-6). Do not confuse this statement with the doctrine that states there is only one way of salvation in all ages. We reject the first but believe and teach the second. The only gospel message in the whole of Scripture, both in the Old Testament and in the New Testament, is that salvation is "by grace through faith." Abraham, and all other Old Testament saints, were all saved by grace through faith in the same gospel message as we are saved today. However, God's one sovereign *purpose* of grace in all ages to save his one elect people and a purely theological temporal *covenant* of grace are not the same things.

TWO: There is one redeemed people of God in all ages under this one covenant of grace. By "redeemed people of God," Covenant Theology means the one true church includes the entire physical nation of Israel, both adults and children along with the New Testament believers and their children. They view the "redeemed nation of Israel" as part of the one true church of God. The Christian church is the same church as Israel with Gentile believers and their children added to it.

THREE: There is one unchanging standard of moral conduct for the one redeemed people of God under the one covenant of grace. If the moral code for a Christian differs in any way from the moral code for an Israelite, then there are two codes of conduct and Covenant Theology's view of law is destroyed. (See John Murray's *Principles of Conduct*.)[16]

Let us again ask the key question: With whom is Christ contrasting himself in the Sermon on the Mount when he says, "But I say unto you"? I would answer, "He is contrasting himself with Moses and the old covenant." However, remember we have kept insisting that *contrasting* is not *contradicting!* I would say that Christ is speaking as the new Lawgiver who replaces Moses in his role as "that Prophet" promised in Deuteronomy 18. Our Lord is laying out the rules for the new kingdom of grace and is contrasting those new laws, based on grace and redemption, with the laws of Moses, based on pure law, for the theocracy of Israel. The new laws make much higher demands because they are given to redeemed saints and not to hard-hearted sinners, as was the case with Israel. Covenant Theology, on the other hand, must

---

[16] John Murray, *Principles of Conduct, Aspects of Biblical Ethics* (Grand Rapids, MI: Eerdmans, 1957) 14–19.

insist that Christ is only contrasting himself with the rabbinical distortions of the law of Moses. To allow Christ to change in any way any of the "eternal unchanging moral law" of God, given to Moses at Sinai, would destroy the very foundation of Covenant Theology's view of law.

I agree that Christ often refutes the Pharisee's distortion of the law of Moses (Matt.15:1-20; 23:1-36). However, he also clearly demonstrates the great difference between the law of Moses that established an earthly theocracy and the laws of grace that govern the body of Christ. Christ, in the Sermon on the Mount, is doing something other than just giving the "true interpretation" of Moses. All of the contrasts he makes are with specific statements recorded in the Old Testament. There is not a single mention in the Sermon on the Mount of any distortion of Moses by a Pharisee. Every statement of contrast is between specific statements by Moses with specific statements of contrast by Christ. There is no textual evidence to support the idea that Christ is correcting rabbinical distortions of Moses. An unbiased reading of the text leads the reader to conclude that our Lord is giving new and higher laws based on grace.

Here are some examples of Covenant Theology's view of Christ's "But I say unto you" statements in the Sermon on the Mount. They are both clear and emphatic. Greg Bahnsen writes:

> Christ's *primary* concern at this point [Matt. 5:17-48] was the validity and meaning of the older Testamental law. From the antitheses listed in verse 21-48 we see that Christ was concerned to show how the meaning of the Law was being distorted (and thus its fine points overlooked).
>
> These radical commands (vv. 21-48) do NOT supersede the older Testamental law; they illustrate and explain it ... In six antitheses between His teaching and the scribal interpretations

Christ demonstrates His confirmation of the older Testamental law ....

So we see in Matthew 5:21-48 examples of how Christ confirms the older Testamental law and reproves the Pharisaical use of it; the antitheses are case law applications of the principle enunciated in Matthew 5:17-20. Christ did not come to abrogate the law; far from it! He confirmed it in full measure, thereby condemning scribal legalism and showing us the pattern of our Christian sanctification [17].

Bahnsen is not alone in this view. A.W. Pink agrees with Bahnsen.

Christ is not here [Matt. 5:28-42] pitting Himself against the Mosaic law, nor is He inculcating a superior spirituality. ... our Lord's design in these verses has been misapprehended, the prevailing but erroneous idea being held that they set forth the vastly superior moral standard of the New Covenant over that which was obtained under Judaism. [18]

Dr. Richard Barcellos's whole book, *In Defense of the Decalogue,* agrees with the above quotations. Barcellos defends Covenant Theology's view of the Ten Commandments as the "unchanging moral law of God." I defend the authority of Christ to be a true Lawgiver. The following quotation from my review of Barcellos summarizes the discussion.

We would claim for our reply that it is a defense of the enduring laws of God *contained* in (but not exhausted by) the Ten Commandments, then expounded and *expanded* by our Lord Jesus Christ, the new lawgiver, in his ministry and later through the inspired epistles of the New Covenant Scriptures. Our basic disagreement with Barcellos has nothing to do with whether the revelation of God's will for his people comes in

---

[17] Greg L. Bahnsen, *Theonomy in Christian Ethics* (Nacogdoches, TX: Covenant Media Press, 2002), 65, 92, 120.

[18] Arthur W. Pink, *An Exposition of the Sermon on the Mount* (Memphis, TN: Bottom of the Hill Publishing, 2011), 85, 98.

clear and concrete commandments, or whether the Ten Commandments are a vital part of that revelation applicable to a child of God today. Our difference is (1) whether Moses is the *greatest lawgiver that ever lived*, including the Lord Jesus Christ himself, or (2) whether Jesus replaced Moses as the new prophet and lawgiver in the very same sense that he replaced Aaron as the new high priest. These two contrary principles underlie the two positions. New Covenant Theology defends Jesus Christ as the new, greater, full, and final lawgiver who replaces Moses. We insist that the laws of Christ, given to the children of the kingdom of grace, make higher demands than those given by God to Israel at Sinai. Our position makes us theological *supernomians*, rather than antinomians as some of our opponents have claimed. Barcellos defends Moses as the greatest lawgiver who ever lived and the laws that God gave him at Sinai are the highest laws ever given.[19]

Walter Chantry, another contemporary writer, makes the Covenant Theology position clear.

> Our Lord Jesus Christ himself did not give a condensed and definitive code of morality. In his great sermon on kingdom righteousness (Matt. 5), the greatest Prophet produced no new standard. He merely gave clear exposition of the old statutes. These were selected, not to make a complete list of duties, but to correct the prevailing misinterpretations of the hour.[20]

Are we justified in asking this question: If Christ is indeed "the greatest Prophet" but he "produced no new standard" of moral duty for believers, then was he really a prophet or was he only a scribe or a rabbi? Why are the above-quoted writers, as well as all those committed to Covenant Theology, so adamant that Christ in no way changed or added to any of the laws of God given to Moses at Sinai? Why do they insist that

---

[19] John G. Reisinger, *In Defense of Jesus, the New Lawgiver* (Frederick, MD: New Covenant Media, 2008), 12, 13.

[20] Walter Chantry, *God's Righteous Kingdom*, (Carlisle, PA: Banner of Truth Trust, 1980), 81.

we must raise Moses above Christ himself in the area of law-giver? The answer is quite simple. They do it for the same reason they make an issue over the Sabbath. If there is even the slightest change in the "moral laws" given to Israel and the "moral laws" given to the church, then we have two different canons of conduct: one for Israel and a different one for the church,[21] but that is impossible in Covenant Theology. There must be a "Christian Sabbath" under the new covenant or Covenant Theology has lost one of its foundation stones. If there are two canons of conduct, one for Israel that includes a weekly Sabbath and another one for the church that sees Christ as the fulfilling and abolishing the Sabbath, then Covenant Theology's view of law is invalid. If we pull the Sabbath commandment out of "THE unchanging moral law," or change in any way any other commandment, then the entire system collapses. This is why churches and preachers of this persuasion are not primarily interested in whether or not

---

[21] John Murray honestly faces and seeks to answer the problem. "Is there, in the sense defined, a biblical ethic? Is there one coherent and consistent ethic set forth in the Bible? Is there not diversity in the Bible, and diversity of a kind that embraces antithetical elements? Are there not in the Bible canons of conduct that are contrary to one another? To be specific: Is there not an antithesis between the canons of conduct sanctioned and approved of God in the Old Testament and those sanctioned and approved of God in the New in respect of certain central features of human behavior? It is a patent fact that the behavior of the most illustrious of Old Testament believers was characterized by practices which are clearly contradictory of the elementary demands of the New Testament ethic. Monogamy is surely a principle of the Christian ethic. Old Testament saints practiced polygamy. In like manner, under the Old Testament divorce was practiced on grounds that could not be tolerated in terms of the explicit provisions of the New Testament revelation. And polygamy and divorce were practiced without overt disapprobation in terms of the canons of behavior which were recognized as regulative in the Old Testament period. *Principles of Conduct* (Grand Rapids, MI: Eerdmans, 1957), 14.

their church members watch football on Sunday as long as they acknowledge that the Sabbath is in force and it is their duty to be "holy." Exactly how they demonstrate their holiness is entirely up to each individual and their personal "Christian liberty."[22]

You will notice that in the quotation above, Bahnsen writes "old<u>er</u> Testament<u>al</u> <u>law</u>" instead of Old Testament. Bahnsen does this to demonstrate as forcefully as possible that there are no such things as real, true, and radically different new and old covenants. There is only one covenant of grace, with an older and a newer version of that one and same covenant. We wonder why the writers of both the Old Testament Scriptures and New Testament Scriptures never once use either the word "older" or the phrase "older Testamental law" when they write about the old and new covenants.

Why does Bahnsen reject the very words that the Holy Spirit used, "old *covenant,*" and instead use the words "older *Testamental* law" that the Holy Spirit never used even once? Does, or does not, the Word of God clearly state in plain words that there is indeed both a new and an old covenant, and further, that the new covenant has replaced and done away with the old covenant in its entirety (Heb. 8:6-13)? Where does the Word of God, even one time, refer to two (an *older* and a *newer*) administrations of one and the same "Testamental law"? Again, we must not confuse what Bahnsen, Pink, and Chantry teach about one *unchanging covenant of grace* with *two administrations* with the theological tenet that God has *one unchanging purpose in sovereign grace* that is administrated differently under different covenants in different ages. We believe the latter and reject the former. Covenant Theology confuses God's single sovereign purpose in grace

---

22 See John G. Reisinger, *The Believer's Sabbath* (Frederick, MD: New Covenant Media, 2002), to help clarify this issue.

with a theological temporal covenant of grace that has no textual evidence in Scripture.

As I mentioned, Bahnsen, Pink, and Chantry are not alone in this "new version of the same covenant" idea. This is standard Covenant Theology. The following is from a theological note in *The Reformation Study Bible* (R.C. Sproul, General Editor) on Genesis 12:3, titled "God's Covenant of Grace."

> As Hebrews 7-10 explains, through Christ God inaugurated a better version of His one eternal covenant with sinners (Heb. 13:20)—a better covenant with better promises (Heb. 8:6)…This better covenant guarantees a better hope than had ever been made explicit by the former version of the covenant …[23]

A careful reading of that statement reveals the confusion involved.

First, we read, "Hebrews 7–10 explains, through Christ God inaugurated a better *version* of His one eternal covenant with sinners." It should be self-evident that God's one eternal covenant with sinners cannot possibly have a "better" version. The text in Hebrews 7-10 nowhere mentions or intimates anything about a better "version" of "the covenant." It specifically speaks of a new, different, and better covenant that replaces an old, different and obsolete covenant. Using the word *version* to modify *covenant* adds to the Word of God and literally changes its meaning.

The Reformation Study Bible immediately follows its "better version" statement by explaining what it means—there is "a better covenant with better promises." Now which is it? Is it a better *version of a former covenant* or is it a *totally new, different and better covenant* than the one it replaces? It cannot be both. *Version* is not a synonym for *covenant*. Is this new covenant better than the old one because the new covenant is based on

---

[23] *The Reformation Study Bible* (Lake Mary, FL: Ligonier Ministries, 2005), 30.

different and better promises? That is exactly what Hebrews 8:6 states. The foundation of the old covenant was based on law and said "do or die." The new covenant is based on grace and says, "It is finished, only believe." That is not a better version of the same covenant; that is a radical and new covenant based on different and better promises.

The same confusion occurs in the next statement—"This better covenant guarantees a better hope than had ever been made explicit by the former version of the covenant." Is there a real new covenant or is there only a newer version of a former covenant? The writer cannot seem to make up his mind. Are we not justified in asking, "Where is this 'former version of the covenant' ever mentioned in Scripture?" I challenge anyone to find where either the Old Testament or Hebrews 7-10 mentions a "better version" of any covenant. The Word of God explicitly says new covenant! It never says new "version" or new "administration" of "one eternal covenant." Textually, a specifically new and radically different covenant totally replaces an old and obsolete covenant. It is that simple! If that is true, then the "one covenant with two administrations or versions" reading of the text is incorrect.

The words "versions" or "administrations" are theological terms, not biblical terms. They are theological necessities produced by logic not biblical facts obtained from exegeting Scripture verses. Covenant Theology will pay lip service to a new covenant, but in reality, they do not actually mean a *new* "covenant" but only a "better version" of one eternal covenant. To keep their theological system intact, they play word games. The Reformation Study Bible quote demonstrates this fact quite clearly. Covenant Theology will speak of a new covenant and in the very same breath deny that it really is a new covenant. It is only a better version, or administration, of that one eternal covenant. There is no true new and different covenant in Covenant Theology!

The blurring of "covenant" into "version" is standard Covenant Theology practice because that is precisely what the *WCF* teaches in Chapter 7, "God's Covenant with Man." The *Confession* states that the new covenant that replaces the old covenant does not "differ in substance," because there is only one covenant of grace. "There are not therefore two covenants of grace, differing in substance, but one and the same, under various dispensations."[24]

Here again we would point out that we whole-heartedly agree that God's one sovereign *purpose* in grace has been administered differently under different covenants. Likewise, we agree there are not two covenants of grace. However, unlike Covenant Theology, we believe that Israel never was under any covenant of grace. If the nation of Israel had been under a covenant of grace, what grounds would God have had for casting her off? Israel was not under the same covenant that the church is.[25] If we are under the same covenant that Israel was under, how can we be sure that God will not cast us off as he did Israel?

Covenant Theology writers often will refer to the old and new covenants as the "Older Covenant of Grace" and the "Newer Covenant of Grace." J. Barton Payne published a book on the Old Testament and titled it *The Older Covenant of Grace*. In reality, in Covenant Theology there is no real new covenant that is different in substance and nature from the old covenant. I repeat; it seems to us that Covenant Theology

---

[24] *Westminster Confession of Faith,* Chapter 7, Section 5.

[25] The individual Israelite who had saving faith was just as much "under grace" for the basis of his salvation as a believer in the church age is. However, the nation, as a nation, was not in any sense "under grace" as the church is. One of the primary differences between Israel and the church is that all of the members of the New Covenant community are true believers (cf. Heb. 9:9-11).

confuses God's one unchanging purpose in grace, which clearly shows there is only one way of saving sinners in all ages, with a non-textual temporal covenant of grace.

Statements like those just quoted from the Reformation Study Bible amaze me. More amazing yet is that Reformed Covenantal Baptists (Dr. Fred Malone's term) are ready to defend vehemently the "one covenant with two administrations" theology so essential to the Covenant Theology of the *Westminster Confession of Faith* and so contrary to historic theology. It is this covenant concept that Reformed Baptist Dr. Richard Barcellos is trying to protect in his book *In Defense of the Decalogue*.

Covenant Theology cannot have a new prophet who replaces Moses as a lawgiver. Christ, as that new Prophet, merely interprets the law that Moses already gave at Sinai, but he does not bring any new revelation about what constitutes true holiness. The Covenant Theology mantra is "Moses will drive you to Christ to be justified and Christ will lead you back to Moses to be sanctified." This clearly runs contrary to the text of Deuteronomy 18:15-18, which demands that someone bring new revelation. Mere interpretation of existing revelation will not fulfill the prophecy in this text.

Moses to Christ,
A Shift in Authority
Chapter 3

In chapter 2 we emphasized that one of our major differences with Covenant Theology is an understanding of the clear prediction that Christ would replace Moses as the new lawgiver. We insist that the Sermon on the Mount is not, as claimed by Covenant Theology, Christ correcting the Pharisees' distortion of Moses. It is Christ contrasting his teaching with the law of Moses. That is exactly what Moses prophesied in Deuteronomy 18:15-19 would happen when Christ the New Covenant Prophet came. Covenant Theology insists that Christ never contrasts his teaching with that of Moses since the law God gave Moses, the Ten Commandments written on stone tablets, is the "eternal unchanging law of God." Many theologians believe that changing the Decalogue in any way is tantamount to changing God. The Decalogue must be the rule of life for all people in all ages.

It is vital that we use the word *contrast* and not the word *contradict*. We totally agree that Christ never in any way says or implies that Moses was wrong in any of the laws he gave. If anyone says Christ claims Moses was in any sense wrong, they are indeed destroying the unity of the Scripture. However, it is clear that the holy, righteous and good law (Rom. 7:12) was never intended by God to be the rule of life for his new covenant church. The Law had a distinct purpose and when that purpose was fulfilled, the holy, just and good law was replaced with a higher more spiritual law, the law of Christ. That biblical fact is clearly set forth prophetically in

Deuteronomy 18:15-19. Look again at that important prophecy.

> *I will raise up for them a Prophet like you from among their brethren, and will put My words in His mouth, and He shall speak to them all that I command Him. And it shall be that whoever will not hear My words, which He speaks in My name, I will require it of him* (Deut. 18:18-19 NKJV).

The new covenant Scriptures leave no room for doubt as to what God meant when he made this promise to Moses. Look at how John understood Moses' prophecy in John 12.

> *Then Jesus cried out and said, "He who believes in Me, believes not in Me but in Him who sent Me. And he who sees Me sees Him who sent Me. I have come as a light into the world, that whoever believes in Me should not abide in darkness. And if anyone hears My words and does not believe, I do not judge him; for I did not come to judge the world but to save the world. He who rejects Me, and does not receive My words, has that which judges him-- the word that I have spoken will judge him in the last day. For I have not spoken on My own authority; but the Father who sent Me gave Me a command, what I should say and what I should speak. And I know that His command is everlasting life. Therefore, whatever I speak, just as the Father has told Me, so I speak"* (John 12:44-50 NKJV).

It is exegetically irresponsible to make either Deuteronomy 18 or John 12 mean that Jesus does not give any new laws, but merely interprets what Moses has said. Let me paraphrase Covenant Theology's understanding of Deuteronomy 18. Bold italics indicate where I have inserted Covenant Theology's understanding into the text:

> *I will raise up for them a Prophet like you from among their brethren, and will put My words **the true interpretation of the words I gave you at Sinai** in His mouth, and He shall speak **interpret the true meaning of** all that I commanded **you** Him. And it shall be that whoever will not hear **His interpretation of** My words **to you**, which He speaks in My name **will repeat and correctly interpret** I will require it of him* (Deut. 18:18-19, revised).

We can do the same thing with John 12: 49, 50:

For I have not spoken on My own authority; but the Father who sent Me gave Me a command, what I should say and what I should speak. And that commandment was to repeat and give the true interpretation of the unchanging law that My Father gave to Moses. And I know that His command is everlasting life. Therefore, whatever I speak is always the same thing as Moses spoke. I am the true and final interpreter of Moses, the greatest lawgiver, just as the Father has told Me, so I speak and interpret the true meaning of Moses' law.

Some may accuse me of caricature, but I think any honest person will see that I have articulated what Bahnsen, Pink, Chantry and Barcellos have clearly expressed, but perhaps not as bluntly, in their writing.

The Object Lesson – the New Covenant Prophet

Mark 9:2-8 records the great object lesson that shows Christ is the new Lawgiver or Prophet who replaces Moses. It is worth noting that Moses did not make it into the land of Canaan during his lifetime because of his outburst of anger, but Mark 9:2-8 proves that he finally made it into Immanuel's land.

After six days Jesus took Peter, James and John with him and led them up a high mountain, where they were all alone. There he was transfigured before them. His clothes became dazzling white, whiter than anyone in the world could bleach them. And there appeared before them Elijah and Moses, who were talking with Jesus. Peter said to Jesus, "Rabbi, it is good for us to be here. Let us put up three shelters—one for you, one for Moses and one for Elijah." (He did not know what to say, they were so frightened.) Then a cloud appeared and enveloped them, and a voice came from the cloud: "This is my Son, whom I love. Listen to him!" Suddenly, when they looked around, they no longer saw anyone with them except Jesus.

As we unpack this text, we begin first with the significance of Moses and Elijah. Moses represents the Law and Elijah represents the Prophets. The phrase "the Law and the Prophets" is a common designation referring to the Old Testament, and Moses and Elijah symbolically portray the Hebrew Scriptures.

Second, verse seven is a direct and deliberate rebuke from God in response to Peter's statement in verse five. Peter makes Moses and Elijah equal to Christ as spokesmen for God and revealers of God's truth and will for his people. God the Father announces that his Son alone is the single and final authority. Moses and Elijah have had their day and are now replaced by Christ. God's Son has replaced the Law and the Prophets as revealer of truth.

Third, a comparison of Mark 9:7, "This is my Son, whom I love. Listen to him!" with Deuteronomy 18:15, "the LORD your God will raise up for you a prophet like me from among your own brothers. You must listen to him" shows a clear and specific promise/fulfillment. The message in the prophecy is clear. You must listen to the new prophet whom I will raise up—you must listen to my Son who is the new and final Prophet. The Mount of Transfiguration is the official announcement from God's own lips that the prophecy of Deuteronomy 18 is fulfilled in Christ. God is announcing the shift of authority from the Law and the Prophets to Christ the New Covenant Prophet. Just as Luther wrote the word *sola*, meaning "alone," beside Romans 3:28, so also we could write the word *sola* beside Mark 9:7. Jesus *alone* is the final authority in the New Covenant age for everything, including ethics and morality. We have either to be spiritually deaf or have theological filters on our ears to miss God's message. Other New Testament passages repeat that message: Luke 16:16, "The law and the prophets were until John ..." and John 1:17, "For the law was given through Moses; grace and truth came through Jesus Christ" are examples.

Fourth, when anyone insists that Christ never adds to or in any way changes the law of God given to Moses, they must gut the New Testament Scripture passages where Christ speaks of "My words" as being the new authority.

Fifth, the *hear him* statement by God indicates, (1) "hear him *alone*," and, (2) "hear him *in contrast* to hearing Moses and Elijah." To deny these implications of *hear him* is to reduce Jesus to the same status as a scribe or rabbi and deny his office as Lawgiver. It is to treat the Sermon on the Mount as the Talmud of Jesus instead of new laws of the new kingdom of grace given by the new King and Lawgiver. It is to reduce Christ to a great, even the greatest, rabbi but nonetheless, still a rabbi with only the authority of an interpreter. Matthew, in his gospel, points out the difference between Jesus and the rabbis in terms of authority. *"When Jesus had finished saying these things* [the Sermon on the Mount], *the crowds were amazed at his teaching, because he taught as one who had authority, and not as their teachers of the law"* (Matt. 7:28). The crowds are amazed, not just because Jesus is the best interpreter they had ever heard, but because he is a different kind of teacher altogether. If we insist that Jesus Christ is not doing something new and inherently different from the other rabbis, then we deny that our Lord is a Lawgiver in his own right who replaces Moses in exactly the same way he replaced Aaron.

Paul, in Ephesians 2:19 and 20, presents additional implications of the object lesson on the Mount of Transfiguration:

> *Consequently, you are no longer foreigners and aliens, but fellow citizens with God's people and members of God's household, built on the foundation of the apostles and prophets, with Christ Jesus himself as the chief cornerstone.*

An important point to establish in this text is to determine to whom Paul refers when he uses the word *prophets*. Almost every commentary on Ephesians written over a hundred years ago will say that the words "apostles and prophets" in this text refer to both the Old Testament and New Testament. It is a reference to the whole Bible. Thirty to fifty years ago, some commentators, like Martyn Lloyd-Jones, said, "The word prophets may be referring to either the Old Testament or the New Testament prophets." Most commentaries today will say that *prophets* in Ephesians 2:19 and 20 must refer to New Testament prophets and cannot mean Old Testament prophets. William Hendriksen is an example. He proves this point beyond question. Here are his comments on Ephesians 2:19 and 20.

> The position that the term prophets as here used refers to the Old Testament bearers of that appellative, such as Moses, Elijah, Isaiah, Jeremiah, etc., (thus Lenski, op. cit., pp. 450-453), is open to serious objections such as the following: (1) Apostles are mentioned first, then prophets; (2) the designation of 'foundation' of the house, a dwelling shared equally by Jew and Gentile, suits the New Testament prophets better than those of the older dispensation; (3) according to 4:8-11, the prophets there mentioned immediately after the apostles, just as here in 2:20, are 'gifts' bestowed on the church by the ascended Christ; hence, prophets of the New Testament era; and (4) 3:5, where the same expression 'apostles and prophets' occurs in a context from which the reference to the prophets of the old dispensation is definitely excluded, would seem to clinch the argument in favor of New Testament prophets.[26]

You may, as I do, find it hard to believe that an avowed Covenant Theologian would make such statements. How Hendriksen can reconcile those comments to his own theological system is beyond me. I admire him for being honest with the words and truth of the text. He argues competently and compellingly that Paul is writing about New Testament prophets and not Old Testament prophets.

---

[26] William Hendrikson, *New Testament Commentary, Ephesians* (Grand Rapids, MI: Baker Book House, 1967) 142.

John Stott goes one step further and shows the biblical and theological implications of Hendrickson's excellent exegesis. What is significant about the definition of the word prophet as New Testament prophet? It is another declaration of the shift of authority from the old covenant to the new covenant. It is another example of discontinuity.

> The reference must again be to a small group of inspired teachers, associated with the apostles, who together bore witness to Christ and whose teaching was derived from revelation (3:5) and was foundational. In practical terms, this means that the church is built on the New Testament Scriptures. They are the church's foundation documents ... The church stands or falls by its loyal dependence on the foundation truths which God revealed to his apostles and prophets, and which are now preserved in the New Testament Scriptures. [27]

Ephesians 2:20 means, as Stott says, that there is a historical shift of authority. The life and worship of the nation of Israel was built on the old covenant Scriptures, but the life and worship of the body of Christ is built on the new covenant Scriptures. The authority for all truth and morality for the nation of Israel was the Law and the Prophets, but now the authority is Jesus Christ, the New Covenant Prophet. Whenever Paul's words in Ephesians 2:20 are minimized or ignored and Moses carries equal (which actually is greater) authority over the conscience of either the church or the individual Christian, there is a clear denial of the unique and final authority of the lordship of Christ in the area of ethics and morality. [28]

---

[27] John Stott, *God's New Society, The Message of Ephesians* (Downers Grove, IL: Inter-Varsity Press, 1979), 107.

[28] For an expanded discussion see my *Christ, Lord and Lawgiver over the Church* (Frederick, MD: New Covenant Media, 1998).

What are the practical implications of what I am saying for the church as a whole and the individual Christian in particular? Is this just much ado about nothing? The practical result in the life of the church and the Christian is a two-tiered system of ethics. As I said earlier, the problem is the lowered standard of biblical holiness in the church. Think carefully about these questions:

If the Sermon on the Mount and the New Covenant Epistles do indeed present a higher and more spiritual standard of holy living than the Law of Moses, what happens if we send a Christian back to Moses to learn ethics and morality? Do we not effectively, in the very name of holiness, lower the actual standard of holiness under which a Christian is to live?

All parties in this debate agree that the major goal of preaching and teaching is to produce holy living among the hearers. The key point of difference among theologians concerns the content of what we preach to the saints to help them live holy lives. One theology says, "Press the law to their conscience" and the other theology says, "Free the conscience from the threat of law and marry it to Christ alone." One theologian will insist that Moses still belongs on the Mount of Transfiguration and the other theologian will insist that Moses has faithfully finished the job God gave him and has replaced him with a greater Prophet.

The bottom line in this discussion is always the authority of the lordship of Christ in relationship to the authority of Moses. Who rules the Christian's conscience, Moses or Christ? Is Moses the final and full lawgiver and Christ merely the true interpreter and enforcer of Moses? Or is Christ the new Lawgiver who supersedes and replaces Moses with higher laws in exactly the same way he replaces Aaron as High Priest? Are Moses and Christ equal authorities over the church's morality and the Christian's conscience? Was Peter correct after all in his desire to build a tabernacle each for Moses, Elijah, and Christ?

Classical Covenant Theology, even if unintentionally, produces a two-tiered system of morality and holiness. Unhappily, Moses occupies the top tier. I do not believe this is their intention, but it is still the result. Let me explain what I mean.

Suppose a married couple comes into a pastor's study for counseling. Their marriage is in trouble. There is no hint that they have broken God's law by committing adultery, but they are none the less contemplating divorce. Do you get the picture? Do you realize what I have just done? I have set you up. I have framed the biblical demands of marriage in terms of a two-tiered ethic. I have defined "God's law" concerning marriage in terms only of sexual immorality and of breaking the seventh commandment. By doing so, I have also implied that whatever other biblical rules of marriage the couple may have violated, those rules are not in the same category as "God's unchanging moral law" written on stone.

It is obvious that one, or both, of these two people have been very unfaithful and disobedient to some things that the Word of God teaches about marriage. However, with a two-tiered system of ethics, you have *real Commandments*, or laws, ten of them in fact, and you also have excellent *spiritual advice* found in the Epistles of the New Testament Scriptures. True, these rules of spiritual advice are biblical, but they are on a lower tier than "God's unchanging moral Law" written on tablets of stone.

We would posit that the couple did indeed break the holy law of God simply because the new covenant Epistles are a vital part of the holy law of God for a Christian. The book of Ephesians is just as much a part of the holy law of God as the Law written in stone in Exodus 20. Every imperative, or commandment, in the New Testament Scriptures is just as much the holy, unchanging, moral law of God for a new covenant believer as the words written on stone at Sinai. However, a two-tiered system of morality cannot treat the "spiritual advice" in Paul's epistles with the same authority as the Tablets of Stone, or the "moral law of God."

What will the Covenant Theology pastor say to this couple? He cannot take them back to "the unchanging moral law of God" written on the Tablets of Stone simply because none of those "unchanging moral laws" were broken. None of the ten directly applies to the present problem since neither party was unfaithful to the Law of God recorded on the stone tables. So, the pastor will go to the Epistles of Paul (the lower tier), and start with the truth of the cross. He will earnestly plead, *on the grounds of redemption, not unchanging law,* that the couple must begin to apply the spiritual principles that Paul delineates. He will assure them that this is the only way to have a happy marriage. In essence, the pastor is saying, "I urge you to apply these biblical principles for the sake of harmony and happiness in your marriage, but whatever you do, do not break God's holy law and commit adultery." The Ten Commandments, called the "moral Law," are the biggies on the top tier and disobedience to them leads to church discipline. Paul's epistles are excellent spiritual advice and disobedience to them leads to more counseling sessions.

If even the moral teaching of Jesus must be interpreted through the grid of Moses, then certainly the teaching of morality by Paul must also be checked with Moses. Is it not a fact, beyond dispute that such a theology cannot allow the words of Paul to carry the same authority over the conscience of a Christian as God's "holy moral law" written on tablets of stone? Must we not also admit unless our conscience is married to a creed, that the cause of this tragic reality is self-evident? If Jesus is not allowed to give any higher laws than Moses gave, then the writing apostles who carry the work of Jesus forward cannot change Moses either. The entire New Testament teaching on morality merely becomes a commentary on Exodus 20:1-17. Mount Sinai is the mountain peak where the full and final word on morality has been given.

What am I saying? Am I suggesting that the laws (good spiritual advice) in the Epistles of Paul are of equal authority with the Ten Commandments (holy, unchanging, moral law) over the conscience of Christians? No, I am not saying that at all. I am saying that Paul's epistles should have a greater authority than Moses. It is impossible, in an experiential sense, for us to make the new covenant teachings of Christ, given by his Spirit, through his apostles, carry the weight of absolute law in either the life of the church or the conscience of an individual believer as long as our theology insists that the highest standard for holiness ever given is the Tablets of Stone.

It is a hollow victory that magnifies Mount Sinai by minimizing the Sermon on the Mount and the Epistles of Paul. You cannot posit a two-tiered ethic, with Moses on the top tier, in your theology without practicing the same thing in everyday life. Moses cannot be lord in your theology of morality and Christ be Lord in your practice of holiness in your daily life!

The issue under discussion deeply affects the doctrine of sanctification. Remember the Bahnsen quotation. "He [Christ] confirmed [the Law] in full measure, thereby condemning scribal legalism and showing us *the pattern of our Christian sanctification.*" Covenant Theology sincerely believes that the only way to produce true holy living is by laying the law on the conscience. The New Testament Scriptures teach that the Christian conscience must be free from the law before the desire for true holiness can even exist. The heart of the question is whether sanctification is by grace or by the law. I would urge anyone struggling with this particular point to read Jerry Bridges' book, *Transforming Grace*.

Law and Grace
Chapter 4

The key text on this subject is the promise made in Deuteronomy 15:15-19. Christ perfectly fulfills that prophecy. He is the promised prophet who would replace Moses in his role of prophet and lawgiver. Christ would "be like" Moses in some ways and very unlike Moses in other ways. The major difference is the authority of Christ to speak with the personal authority of God the Son. Moses, and all other prophets, must say, "Thus saith the Lord," but our Lord alone can say, "But I say unto you."

The whole subject of the relationship of law and grace is involved in understanding the fulfillment of the prophecy of Deuteronomy 15:15-19. A short review of God using Moses as a mediator in establishing the old covenant with the children of Israel at Mount Sinai will not only help us understand Christ as our New Covenant Prophet, but it will also help in understanding the larger issue of law and grace. It is essential that we have a clear understanding of the radical difference between the covenant God made with Abraham and the covenant he made with the children of Israel at Mount Sinai. This will involve seeing exactly how Jacob's (Israel) children become the covenant nation of God and how Moses became that nation's Lawgiver.

First, we must distinguish between Israel as a nation, or body politic, and the children of Israel as merely the children of Jacob. The terms *"children of Israel"* and *"nation of Israel"* will become synonymous but they did not begin that way. Jacob's children were not a nation—a body politic—prior to God entering into a special and specific covenant with them at Mount Sinai. They were not a nation—a body politic—when Joseph brought them down to Egypt nor did they become a nation while in Egypt. The children of Jacob became a *nation* at Mount Sinai. It was there that Jacob's children officially became a nation or a body politic. Up to that point in time the children of Israel were not yet constituted a nation or body politic, they were merely the children of Jacob (Israel). Abraham never became a physical nation even though he was the grandfather of Jacob, the man who became the father of the nation. Neither Abraham, Isaac, nor Jacob was a prophet, priest or king. The three offices of prophet, priest and king are associated with the nation of Israel and her covenant with God. The covenant at Sinai that constituted Israel as a nation is not the same as the covenant with Abraham.

The first use of the word "nation" in Scripture is God's promise to Abraham.

> *The Lord had said to Abram, "Leave your country, your people and your father's household and go to the land I will show you.*
>
> *"I will make you into a great nation*
>> *and I will bless you;*
> *I will make your name great,*
>> *and you will be a blessing* (Gen.12:1-2).

God promised Abraham that he would not only have a seed, he would become the father of many nations. His son Isaac, born to Sarah, would be the seed line that would bring forth the Messiah. His grandson Jacob would not only become a great physical nation, he would also become the spiritual seed that constitutes the spiritual nation, the true church of Christ. Ishmael, Abram's son by Hagar, Sarah's handmaid, would also become a great nation[29] but would not in any

---

[29] For a study of Abraham's seeds see my *Abraham's Four Seeds* (Frederick, MD: New Covenant Media, 1998).

sense be a spiritual nation as was Jacob (Israel). Hagar mothered a true son to Abraham named Ishmael but both mother and child were "cast out" without receiving the inheritance (Gen. 21:10, cf. Gal. 4:30).

The first use of the word "Israel" in Scripture is when God changed Jacob's name from Jacob to "Israel."

> ... *"Your name will no longer be Jacob, but Israel, ...* (Gen 32:28).

The children of Israel, as a people, are promised by God at Mount Sinai that if they would obey the covenant he was about to make with them, they would become a holy and special nation, a body politic, bound by special covenant to God. God proceeds to enter into this special covenant with the children of Israel at Mount Sinai in Exodus 20.

> *In the third month after the Israelites left Egypt — on the very day — they came to the Desert of Sinai. After they set out from Rephidim, they entered the Desert of Sinai, and Israel camped there in the desert in front of the mountain.*
>
> *Then Moses went up to God, and the Lord called to him from the mountain and said, "This is what you are to say to the house of Jacob and what you are to tell the people of Israel: 'You yourselves have seen what I did to Egypt, and how I carried you on eagles' wings and brought you to myself. Now if you obey me fully and keep my covenant, then out of all nations you will be my treasured possession. Although the whole earth is mine, you will be for me a kingdom of priests and a holy nation.' These are the words you are to speak to the Israelites"* (Ex. 19:1-6).

Israel never became the promised spiritual holy nation simply because she never kept the covenant terms. Exodus 19:4-6 is totally misunderstood by covenant theologians. Their typical interpretation of these verses is this: Exodus 19:4-6 is the preamble to the covenant. In verse 4, God reminds the Israelites that they are a redeemed people "under grace." Covenant Theology insists that the covenant at Sinai was a gracious covenant made with a "redeemed" by which they mean "justified" people. It totally ignores the big "if" and the "then" in verse 5.[30] They fail to see the covenant at Sinai was a conditional covenant. Israel was indeed a people redeemed by blood, but it was not spiritual redemption by Christ's blood. It was a physical redemption from Egypt by animal blood. Israel becoming a "kingdom of priests" and a "holy nation" was totally dependent upon their keeping the covenant terms of Exodus 20, which they never did. The covenant at Sinai was without question a legal covenant of works conditioned on Israel's obedience to the covenant terms. The words "if you will obey" and "then I will" cannot be made to mean "I will whether you do or not." The covenant at Sinai was without question a conditional covenant. Language cannot be more explicit. God said, "If you obey me fully and keep my covenant, then [and only then] … you will be for me a kingdom of priests and a holy nation." They did become a "holy"[31] (meaning separate) physical nation, but they did not become a "holy," (meaning spiritual) nation where all of the members in the nation were regenerate saints. Failing to see this is one of the tragic mistakes of covenant theologians.

---

[30] **Exodus 19:5: If you obey.** Compare 1 Pet. 2:9; Rev. 1:6; Rev. 5:10. What under law was conditional is, under grace, freely given to every believer. The "if" of verse 5 is the essence of law as a method of divine dealing, and the fundamental reason why the law "made nothing perfect" (Heb. 7:18, 19; compare Rom. 8:3). To Abraham the promise preceded the requirement; at Sinai the requirement preceded the promise. In the New Covenant the Abrahamic order is followed. See Hebrews. 8:8-12. *Scofield Reference Bible,* (New York: Oxford University Press, 2003), 113.

[31] The word "holy" means separated unto God. Israel was separated from all other nations, and belonged exclusively to God as a nation. Unfortunately very few Israelites were ever "holy" in the sense of being sanctified unto God in personal salvation. "Holy" does not always mean moral purity.

They totally fail to see the relationship of the old and new Covenants. They read a new covenant meaning of the great redemptive words back into the old covenant nation of Israel.

Israel, as a nation, was loved as no other nation, but it was not the same redemptive love with which Christ loved the Church. Israel, as a nation, was sovereignly chosen to be God's people but that choice, or election, was not the same as the Church being chosen unto everlasting life. Israel, as a nation was called out of bondage to Egypt but that is not the same as the spiritual calling (regeneration) that effectually calls us out of bondage to sin and unites us to Christ. Israel, as a nation, was redeemed by blood, but it was the blood of an animal not the blood of Christ. It was physical redemption not spiritual redemption.

It is a grievous error to treat the redemptive words "loved, chosen, called and redeemed" the same when applied to Israel *as a nation* as they are when they are used of the church. Every single Israelite could say, "God *loved* me with a *special love* and sovereignly *chose me*. He *redeemed me* with a blood sacrifice and *called me* out of Egypt." Every Israelite could say all of those things and still be as lost as the Devil simply because all of those things were physical and applied only to physical Israel. Every member of the body of Christ can say all of those things in the certainty that they are saved and eternally secure in Christ. The one thing every new covenant believer can add to that list of things is, "I am justified." Very few Israelites could add, "I am justified." Hebrews 3:8-11 and 4:1-2 describe the same people who were "loved, chosen, called and redeemed" in the nation of Israel. Israel was a *type* of the church but must never be treated as the true redeemed justified people of God. Not a single person who is "loved, chosen, called and redeemed" in the new covenant meaning of those words was ever lost. Most of the physical nation of

Israel that was "loved, chosen, called and redeemed" was lost.

The whole subject of the nature of the covenant at Sinai needs to be examined in another book, but my main concern here is to show that Israel's nationhood began at Sinai and was based on a covenant of works. Israel never received the blessings promised in that covenant and was disowned as a nation when they crucified their Messiah. The church, including saved Jews and Gentiles, has received the specific blessings promised in Exodus 19:4-6 (see 1 Peter 2:5-10). The church is the true holy nation, God's peculiar possession, and all her members are regenerate priests.

Let us compare the covenant God made with Abraham and his seed with the covenant he made with the children of Israel at Mount Sinai. In one sense, God's covenant with Abraham included all of his seed, but in another sense his seed only included Jacob and his children. Ishmael, the father of the Arabs, was just as much a true son of Abraham as was Isaac. Ishmael is called Abraham's son, and he was circumcised on the same day that Abraham was circumcised. *Abraham and his son Ishmael were both circumcised on that same day.* (Gen. 17:26). Ishmael was promised every specific blessing, except being in the seed line for the Messiah, that Isaac was given. *And as for Ishmael, I have heard you: I will surely bless him; I will make him fruitful and will greatly increase his numbers. He will be the father of twelve rulers, and I will make him into a great nation* (Gen. 17:20). Ishmael was Abraham's true son just as much as was Isaac. Ishmael was Abraham's true physical seed but not his spiritual seed. Scripture is very explicit on this point.

As I mentioned, Abraham was not a prophet, a priest or a king. Those three offices were instituted in the nation of Israel and were fulfilled in the church. All three offices are clearly types of Christ. Dispensationalism sees Christ in the priestly work of Aaron, especially in his tabernacle ministry. The Plymouth Brethren have given us some of the most Christ exalting studies in their messages on Aaron's ministry in and for the church that you will ever read. I have spent many delightful hours with Charles Henry Mackintosh, Ironside and their kinsmen. Likewise, these men have no trouble seeing Moses as "that prophet" as a clear type of Christ fulfilled in the Gospels; however, when they come to the prophets all they can see is the Jews inheriting the land in a future millennium. Israel is not a *type* of the true people of God in dispensationalism; they *are* the true people of God.

Dispensationalism believes the church is a parenthesis in God's eternal purposes. Israel has been likened to a train that has been taken off the main line and placed on a sidetrack. The church is presently on the main track. At the second coming of Christ, the church will be raptured, and the Jews will again be on the main track. At that time God will once again take up special dealings with Israel and will fulfill his promises concerning the promised kingdom. The kingdom promised to Israel in the Old Testament was offered to them by Christ at his first coming, but they rejected him as the promised Messiah. The kingdom was "postponed" until the second coming.

One of the synonyms for the word *parenthesis* is "afterthought' and another one is "digression." Dispensationalism sees the purpose of God made known and worked out in his dealings with the nation of Israel. It is believed that our Lord came to establish the Kingdom of God on earth with the Jewish nation being the head of all the nations. Christ would rule on David's throne. Jerusalem would be the capital of the world. Older dispensationalism believes the temple described in Ezekiel 40–47 will be rebuilt, and both the Aaronic priesthood and the sacrifices will be revived.

Early dispensationalism also insisted that there were two new covenants, one for Israel and one for the church. They believed the new covenant in Hebrews was made with Israel. If this covenant included the Gentiles, it was felt it would weaken premillennialism. Progressive dispensationalism, a recent modification of dispensationalism, insists, on the grounds of Hebrews, that the new covenant was not only made with Israel, but also included the church. Some dispensationalists, and also some non-dispensationalists, feel that the Progressives are inconsistent and should not call themselves dispensationalists. I do not agree with either the early or the progressive dispensationalists. It is quite clear to me that the new covenant was not in any sense made with Israel; it was made with the church. It was made with the people for whom Christ died; it was made to replace the old covenant; and it was to be remembered by the church in this gospel age (1 Cor. 11:23-26).

Jewish believers living in the gospel age are part of the group redeemed body of Christ. Christ is their Prophet; Priest and King, just as he is my Prophet, Priest and King. There is not a Prophet, Priest and King for saved Jews and another Prophet, Priest and King for the church. We simply must understand that when Christ fulfilled the Old Testament promises of the new covenant, all the distinctions between Jew and Gentile were forever abolished. There was a very clear difference between Jew and Gentile under the Old Covenant, but all of those distinctions are done away in Christ.

Two things happened with the coming of the Holy Spirit on the Day of Pentecost. First, the believing Gentiles, by being baptized into the body of Christ, were raised to a place of absolute equality with the believing Jews (cf. Gal. 3:26-29). Second, the unbelieving Jew was lowered to a place of absolute equality with the "Gentile dog."

There is one story line in the Bible. It begins in Genesis 1:1 with God as Creator. When sin entered the world, the story line announced God's response and goal. God's goal was to choose an "election of grace" from among the sinful children of Adam. A coming Redeemer is promised who will undo what Satan did. He is called "the seed of the woman." The Scripture from Genesis 3:15 sets forth God's reaching his goal and saving the sinners he sovereignly chose. The story line tells of a man named Abraham being sovereignly called by God to be the father of the seed line that will finally bring forth the promised seed of the woman. Abraham's great grandchildren, the children of Jacob, wind up in Egypt in slavery to Pharaoh and the Egyptians. God remembers his covenant with Abraham and sends a man named Moses to deliver the sons of Jacob from their bondage to the Egyptians.

At this point the story line on the surface seems to either end or be put on the shelf temporally, and a new story line seems to begin. In this case, the appearance is wrong. God enters into a special and specific covenant at Sinai. The terms of this covenant made at Sinai with Moses as the Mediator was different in nature from the covenant made with Abraham. The children of Israel become a theocratic nation and are promised that if they will obey his covenant made with them at Sinai, they would receive the following blessings. They would be a "peculiar treasure," "kingdom of priests" and a "holy nation." When the people are confronted with the covenant terms, they unanimously agree to keep the covenant terms.

> Now if you obey me fully and keep my covenant, then out of all nations you will be my treasured possession. Although the whole earth is mine, you will be for me a kingdom of priests and a holy nation.' These are the words you are to speak to the Israelites."
>
> So Moses went back and summoned the elders of the people and set before them all the words the Lord had commanded him to speak.

The people all responded together, "We will do everything the Lord has said." So Moses brought their answer back to the Lord (Ex. 19).

How radically different are the terms of the covenant made with Israel at Sinai and the covenant made with Abraham. John Stott has given an excellent summary of the difference between the religion of Abraham and the religion of Moses.

> God's dealings with Abraham and Moses were based on two different principles. To Abraham He gave a promise ('I will show you a land … I will bless you …', Gen. 12:1- 2). But to Moses he gave the law, summarized in the Ten Commandments. 'These two things (as I do often repeat),' comments Luther, 'to wit, the law and the promise, must be diligently distinguished. For in time, in place, and in person, and generally in all other circumstances, they are separate as far asunder as heaven and earth …' Again, 'unless the Gospel be plainly discerned from the law, the true Christian doctrine cannot be kept sound and uncorrupt.' What is the difference between them? In the promise to Abraham God said, 'I will … I will … I will'. But in the law of Moses God said, 'Thou shalt … thou shalt not …'. The promise sets forth a religion of God –God's plan, God's grace, God's initiative. But the law sets forth a religion of man– man's duty, man's works, and man's responsibility. The promise (standing for the grace of God) had only to be believed. But the law (standing for the works of men) had to be obeyed. God's dealings with Abraham were in the category of 'promise,' 'grace' and 'faith'. But God's dealing with Moses was in the category of 'law,' 'commandments' and 'works.'[32]

We have been insisting there is only one story line and one ultimate goal of redemption in Scripture, and now we are saying the religion of Moses and the religion of Abraham are different. The nature of the Abrahamic covenant and the nature

---

[32] 4 John R.W. Stott, *The Message of Galatians*, (Leicester, England: Inter-Varsity Press, 1968), 86-87. The passages from Luther which Stott quotes are from Luther's *Commentary on the Epistle to the Galatians* published by James Clark

of the Mosaic covenant are indeed radically different, but both covenants serve the same goal and are part of the same story line. Israel's brash response of assurance that they could keep the terms of the covenant given at Sinai shows how self-righteous they were. They should have said, "Lord, that is a good and fair covenant, and you have every right to demand its terms of perfect obedience. However, you know and we know that we cannot keep those terms, and we will be dead before the sun goes down." The Mosaic covenant was designed by God to kill all hope of salvation by works and push the sinner to faith in the faith/grace covenant made with Abraham. The Abrahamic covenant was permanent, and the Mosaic covenant was temporary. The law was in force "until the seed of Abraham, the Messiah, came" (Gal 3:19).

The dispensationalist is correct in asserting that there is a parenthesis in Scripture. They just have the parenthesis around the wrong time, wrong place and wrong people. The nation of Israel is the parenthesis- "Long ago, at many times and in many ways, God spoke to our fathers by the prophets …" (Heb. 1:1). In contrast the nature of the church is not parenthetical, "but in these last days he has spoken to us by his Son" (Heb. 1:2) and, "This is my beloved Son, with whom I am well pleased; listen to him" [for he is a prophet superior to Moses and Elijah] (Matt.17:5b).

Christ,
Our New Covenant High Priest
Chapter 5

Hebrews 8:6 is one of the most important verses in the Book of Hebrews, actually in the whole New Testament, for giving us a summary of New Covenant Theology. Hebrews 8:1 informs us that this section is a statement of summary and review.

> *The point of what we are saying is this: We do have such a high priest, who sat down at the right hand of the throne of the Majesty in heaven,* (Heb. 8:1).

New covenant believers have, in our Lord Jesus Christ, the very Priest we need. He has accomplished and forever finished the work that Aaron could never have accomplished. Our High Priest has entered the Most Holy Place and has taken up permanent residence there. He has also made it possible that we poor sinners can also enter that same Most Holy Place at any time of any day or night. We have been given a "perfect clearance and total acceptance pass" into his Father's presence (Rom. 5:1-3). The Lord Jesus Christ, acting as our older brother and representative, has forever accomplished what Aaron and the blood of millions of bulls and goats could never accomplish.

Hebrews 8:6 is a summary statement of three comparisons. The verse compares two priestly ministries, two different covenants and two sets of promises upon which the two covenants are based. These three comparisons demonstrate why Aaron's priestly ministry failed and Christ's priestly ministry succeeds. I have added numbers to the following quotation in order to emphasize the three comparisons.

> But the (1) *ministry Jesus has received is as superior to theirs as the* (2) *covenant of which he is mediator is superior to the old one, and it is founded on* (3) *better promises* (Heb. 8:6).

This verse is vital to any discussion of Christ as our High Priest. The writer of Hebrews sets forth three distinct comparisons of "better" things to show why the new covenant, set forth in verses 7-11 as the fulfillment of the prophecy of the new covenant in Jeremiah 31:31-34, was so essential and is so superior. These three contrasts provide the sum and substance not only of the Book of Hebrews but also of (1) the heart of the religion of the new covenant compared to the religion of the old covenant, or the basic difference between Judaism and Christianity; and (2) the vital difference between the old and new covenants as covenants. Each comparison grows out of the previous comparison, and all three are straightforward and uncomplicated.

First, *our Lord performs a "better ministry" than Aaron*. The obvious question raised by such a statement is this: "Why is Christ's ministry as High Priest so much better than Aaron's ministry?" The answer: Christ's ministry is better than Aaron's ministry because it is based on a "better covenant." The next obvious question then is this: "Why is the new covenant that Christ established so much better than the old covenant that it replaced?" The answer: Because it is based upon "better promises." That leads to the third question: "What are those better promises and why are they so much better?" The answer: The old covenant under which Aaron ministered promised life on the grounds of obedience to the law and the new covenant under which Christ ministers says "it is finished, only believe." The old covenant is based on works and the new covenant is based on grace. The old covenant was deliberately designed to be a "killing covenant." The stated purpose of that covenant was to convict sinners of their guilt and drive them to the Abrahamic covenant to be justified by faith.

All of the three statements are quite clear. We who live under the new covenant have the benefits of a better ministry that was accomplished under a better covenant based on better promises. To identify the nature, purpose, and function of the two contrasted covenants is to understand the biblical relationship of law and grace. Immediately upon making these three comparisons and drawing out the logical meaning and implications of them, the writer of Hebrews reminds us of why the old covenant had to be discarded (Heb.8:7-8.). The old covenant could not meet the sinner's need. It could not effect justification. None of Aaron's work could bring the sinner into God's presence. The writer of Hebrews then quotes Jeremiah 31:31-34 to prove that the change of covenants that was necessary in order for God to accomplish his redemptive purpose was clearly prophesied in the Old Testament Scriptures. This new covenant that was prophesied was God's intended purpose ever since eternity began and was made known at the dawn of sin in Genesis 3:15. Israel and the Mosaic covenant were never intended to be permanent. They were announced as ending when Christ came. As we noted in the preceding chapter, the nation of Israel and the religion of Judaism upon which it was based, was a parenthesis in God's one unchaining redemptive purpose of sovereign grace for his one elect people.

> For if there had been nothing wrong with that first covenant, no place would have been sought for another. But God found fault with the people and said: "The days are coming, declares the Lord, when I will make a new covenant with the people of Israel and with the people of Judah. It will not be like the covenant I made with their ancestors when I took them by the hand to lead them out of Egypt, because they did not remain faithful to my covenant, and I turned away from

them, declares the Lord. This is the covenant I will establish with the people of Israel after that time, declares the Lord. I will put my laws in their minds and write them on their hearts. I will be their God, and they will be my people. No longer will they teach their neighbor, or say to one another, 'Know the Lord,' because they will all know me, from the least of them to the greatest. For I will forgive their wickedness and will remember their sins no more." By calling this covenant "new," he has made the first one obsolete; and what is obsolete and outdated will soon disappear (Heb. 8:7-13).

Any attempt to exegete Jeremiah 31:31-34 without looking at how a new covenant apostle understood that specific prophecy is simply not good hermeneutics, yet this is just what most covenant theologians do. We must not start with Jeremiah, but with how the writer of Hebrews understood Jeremiah. This means that we do not first establish a rigid meaning of Jeremiah 31:31-34, and then make the Book of Hebrews fit into that interpretation. We first understand the theological point that the writer to the Hebrews is making and then ask why he chose to use Jeremiah 31:31-34 to prove that point. This is another clear example of the basic difference in our hermeneutics from that of both Covenant Theology and dispensationalism. This example demonstrates what we mean when we insist that the new covenant Scriptures must interpret the old covenant Scriptures and not the other way around.

It is impossible to understand a comparison if we do not understand both of the things being compared. For instance, if I were to say to you, "Oranges are much sweeter than lemons" and you had never tasted a lemon, my statement would be meaningless. For my statement to make sense you must know what both a lemon and orange taste like. If the writer of Hebrews exalts the ministry of Christ as *better* than the ministry of Aaron, and we do not have a clear picture of, (1) exactly what Aaron's ministry was; (2) why that ministry failed;

and, (3) why the Old Covenant, upon which Aaron's entire ministry was based, had to be replaced with a new and better covenant instead of just patched up, then we cannot understand passages like Jeremiah 31 and Hebrews 8. There is no clear understanding of the greatness of the new covenant until there is a clear understanding of the inherent weakness of the old covenant.

First, we must ask, "Exactly what was Aaron's ministry as high priest?" His greatest single duty was to make sacrifice for the people and then make intercession for them as he sprinkled the mercy seat with animal blood on the Day of Atonement. Hebrews 5:1 states that Aaron "offered gifts and sacrifice for sins." He represented Israel before God with a blood sacrifice and then represented them in intercession. This two-fold ministry of sacrifice and intercession is co-extensive. Aaron prays only for those for whom he shed blood and made intercession. Aaron did not offer any lambs for the Egyptians, nor did he pray for the Philistines. The same is true under the new covenant. Christ died for and prayed for his own elect people. He died for his sheep and prays for those same sheep. How could he state this more clearly?

> I am the good shepherd. The good shepherd lays down his life for the sheep (John 10:11).

> I pray for them. I am not praying for the world, but for those you have given me, for they are yours (John 17:9).

Was Aaron's ministry successful? Did his efforts of sacrifice and intercession pay the sinner's debt and cleanse his conscience from sin? Was Aaron able to bring the sinner into the presence of God "without fear"? The answer to all of these questions is no. However, we must quickly add that the failure to accomplish these things was not because of any sin or lack of either effort or faith on Aaron's part. He used, correctly and in good faith, every means that was available to him to do his job. So why does Jesus prevail in his priestly work and succeed in performing the same functions in which Aaron failed? Our Lord, like Aaron, also offers a sacrifice and makes intercession. However, unlike Aaron, Christ can and does bring the sinner, without fear and with a clear conscience, into the presence of the thrice-holy God. Why does Christ's one offering of blood and his intercession on the ground of that blood accomplish what all of Aaron's offerings of shed blood and his prayers could never effect in a single instance. Both Aaron and Christ pleaded with God on the ground of the blood they shed. Why did one succeed and the other fail?

Part of the answer is given in Hebrews 10 when the writer reminds us of the great difference between an animal's blood and the blood of Christ. However, in Hebrews 8 he uses a different angle to make the same point: that which makes the intercession of Christ effective is not just the better blood that was shed; it also involves the "better" covenant that his once-for-all sacrifice established. Christ's ministry is successful because of the "better covenant" from which he ministers. The *covenant terms*, not just the *kind of blood*, make all the difference. We must see that the blood established the new covenant and the new covenant terms were based on grace while the old covenant terms were based on works.

This leads to the second of the three comparisons in Hebrews 8:6, which begs us to ask, "Why is this new covenant that Christ administers so much better than the covenant under which Aaron ministered? What is the weakness of the old covenant upon which Aaron's ministry was based, and what are the strengths of the new covenant from which Christ ministers?" The writer immediately answers; "The new covenant is based on 'better promises' than the old covenant." If the two covenants were based on the same promises, then Hebrews 8:6 would not make sense. If, as Covenant Theology insists, the new covenant and the old covenant are the same in "nature and substance," then they are not substantially different at all, and again, Hebrews 8:6 becomes words without meaning. If there is not a radically new, totally different and very distinctly better covenant based on new, different, and better promises or better terms than the old covenant was based upon, then, I repeat, the words have lost their meaning. A failure to interpret Jeremiah's prophecy in the light of the Book of Hebrews highlights the different views of the message in Hebrews.

We insist that there was nothing at all bad or wrong with either the old covenant or Aaron as a priest. The old covenant terms were not unfair or too rigid, but, on the contrary, they were "holy, just and good." The old covenant failed simply because it could not produce the very necessary things that are guaranteed in the new covenant. That is what Jeremiah 31:31-34 is all about. The main point of the promise in Jeremiah 31:31-34 is not that God is going to tattoo the Ten Commandments on a new covenant believer's heart nor is it that God is going to write a 'new and different set of rules' on the heart. It is neither of those things. The glory and expectation of the promises in the new covenant, as promised in Jeremiah 31, is that our blessed Savior is going to accomplish what Aaron and the law covenant given through Moses never could accomplish. Christ is going to affect inwardly what Aaron and the law covenant never could accomplish. Jeremiah 31:31-34, as can be seen from Hebrews 8 and 10, is not a law-centered passage, but it is a *Christ-centered passage*. John MacArthur is correct when he comments on Hebrews 8:10:

> The New Covenant will have a different sort of law—an internal not an external law. Everything under the old economy was primarily external. Under the Old Covenant obedience was out of fear of punishment. Under the New it is to be out of adoring love and worshiping thanksgiving. Formerly God's law was given on stone tablets and was to be written on wrists

and foreheads and doorposts as reminders (Deut. 6:8, 9). Even when the old law was given, of course, it was intended to be in His people's hearts (Deut. 6:6). But the people could not write on their hearts like they could write on their doorposts. And at this time the Holy Spirit, the only changer of hearts, was not yet given to believers. Now, however, the Spirit writes God's law in the minds and hearts of those who belong to him. In the New Covenant true worship is internal, not external, real, not ritual (cf. Ezek. 11:19-20, 36:26, 27; John 14:17).[33]

I ask again, why did Aaron's ministry fail? What was it that he could not effectually accomplish? In a nutshell, Aaron and the priests from his line could not meet the just and holy demands of the covenant terms, the Ten Commandments written on the tables of the covenant housed in the Ark of the Covenant. The blessings promised in that covenant (Ex. 19:5- 6) depended on compliance with the covenant terms written on the tables of the covenant. Neither Aaron nor the sinner could meet those terms. 1) They could not obey the covenant terms and earn the life that was promised, and 2) once the covenant terms were broken, they could not bring a sacrifice that could pay for the sin and satisfy both God's holy character and the sinner's conscience. Aaron's inability to effect entrance into God's presence had nothing to do with his godliness or his consistency and perseverance. He did all he could do and all that was expected of him. His ministry still failed and had to be replaced. Hebrews 8:7 does not say, or imply, "because Aaron failed to faithfully perform his work." The real problem is the old covenant terms and the sinner's inability to meet them. Jesus succeeds in the same ministry where Aaron failed. The new covenant constantly emphasizes that Christ

---

[33] John MacArthur, Jr., *The MacArthur New Testament Commentary, Hebrews* (Chicago: Moody Press, 1983), 215.

"finished" the work of redemption. He offered a "once for-ever" sacrifice that satisfied God's covenant terms.

> *How much more, then, will the blood of Christ, who through the eternal Spirit offered himself unblemished to God, cleanse our consciences from acts that lead to death, so that we may serve the living God! For this reason Christ is the mediator of a new covenant, that those who are called may receive the promised eternal inheritance — now that he has died as a ransom to set them free from the sins committed under the first covenant (Heb. 9:14-15).*

> *For Christ did not enter a man-made sanctuary that was only a copy of the true one; he entered heaven itself, now to appear for us in God's presence. Nor did he enter heaven to offer himself again and again, the way the high priest enters the Most Holy Place every year with blood that is not his own. Then Christ would have had to suffer many times since the creation of the world. But now he has appeared once for all at the end of the ages to do away with sin by the sacrifice of himself. Just as man is destined to die once, and after that to face judgment, so Christ was sacrificed once to take away the sins of many people; and he will appear a second time, not to bear sin, but to bring salvation to those who are waiting for him (Heb. 9:24-28).*

It has been noted that there were no chairs in the tabernacle because the priestly work of sacrifice was never finished. After our Lord made his once-for-all-time sacrifice, he "sat down" because his sacrificial work was done.

> *After the Lord Jesus had spoken to them, he was taken up into heaven and he sat at the right hand of God (Mark 16:19; cf. Heb. 8:1).*

We have looked at the first of the three comparisons in Hebrews 8:6. We have seen how the first comparison insists that Christ's ministry of High Priest is better than Aaron's ministry. We will now look at the second comparison.

The second comparison in Hebrews 8:6 is between the two covenants. The writer states that the primary reason Christ's ministry succeeded where Aaron's ministry failed is because Christ's ministry as High Priest is based on a better covenant.

Everything depends on the nature of the covenant under which a priest ministers. Christ succeeds where Aaron failed simply because of Aaron's inability to meet the terms of the covenant under which he ministered. Our Lord perfectly fulfills the demands of the old covenant and then establishes a new and better covenant based on better terms. The new covenant under which Christ ministered is based on grace, but the old covenant under which Aaron ministered was based on works. The efficacy of the sacrifice and the intercession can only be as effective as the covenant under which that work is done. What was needed was a new covenant not merely a new administration of the same covenant. What was the major weakness in the old covenant that necessitated it being totally replaced with a new and better covenant? The answer is quite simple. Aaron could not meet the terms of the old covenant for either himself or for those he represented.

First of all, Aaron could not present to God the holy, sinless, law-keeping, righteous life that the old covenant terms justly demanded. Aaron was a sinner who represented other sinners. He could not provide for himself or for those he represented the perfect righteous life that the "just, good, holy" law covenant demanded, nor could he offer an acceptable sacrifice that could pay the sinner's debt to a holy God. The people Aaron represented, along with Aaron himself, were under the curse of God because they had broken the terms of the covenant, written both on the tablets of the covenant housed in the Ark of the Covenant and in the book of the covenant (Ex. 24:7-8) and sealed with blood.

Secondly, once those covenant terms were broken, that law covenant demanded an acceptable sacrifice to pay for sin. Aaron could no more bring such a sacrifice than he could have brought a righteous sinless life. He could make no true atonement for sin any more than he could earn life by obedience. All he could do was sacrifice an animal and sprinkle its blood on the altar and plead with God to "cover the sin" with the animal's blood until One came who could and would make a true atonement. Our Lord accomplished both of the things that Aaron could not accomplish. He obeyed the law and earned the righteousness that it promised, and then he endured its just curse on the Cross. His righteous life is imputed to all for whom he died just as the sin of those same people is imputed to Christ and fully paid for by him on the cross.

I trust the reader has begun to see the truth of the glory of the new covenant. We have looked at why Christ's ministry as our High Priest is so much better than Aaron's ministry as High Priest. Christ's ministry is based on a better covenant. We now look at the third comparison in Hebrews 8:6.

The third comparison is between the different promises upon which the two covenants rest. Again the writer answers the logical question raised by the second comparison. Why is the new covenant from which Christ ministers so much better than the covenant from which Aaron ministers? The answer is the third comparison. Christ's ministry is better than Aaron's because the old covenant from which Aaron ministered was totally inferior to the new covenant. The old covenant is inferior because it is based on inferior promises. Both covenants promised eternal life but the old covenant required the sinner to obey the law in order to earn the promised life. The new covenant assures the poor sinner that Christ has earned the promised life for us. Aaron could only give sinners a temporary relief. He could not offer a sacrifice that paid for sin and guilt. The covering only lasted for one year, and then there must be another Day of Atonement.

We must remember that there was no real atonement for sin until the cross. That is the first time that sin was actually punished. Every drop of animal blood on the old covenant altars was like an 'I owe you' note. At Calvary, our Lord picked up and paid in full every one of those 'IOUs.' Someone has said, "The old covenant believer was 'saved on credit." We need to clearly understand the nature, function and promises upon which the old covenant was based before we can understand why that old covenant had to be replaced with a new and better covenant. The old covenant is the covenant made with the nation of Israel at Mount Sinai. It was a covenant based on works. It was based on a big "if." IF the Israelite obeyed the terms of the covenant in the Ark of the Covenant, THEN they would receive the blessings promised in the covenant.

> *Now if you obey me fully and keep my covenant, then out of all nations you will be my treasured possession. Although the whole earth is mine, you will be for me a kingdom of priests and a holy nation'* (Ex. 19:5-6).

No child of Adam could keep those terms thus all were condemned under the terms of that covenant. The blessings of the new covenant are established on Gospel terms. They are not based on works but on grace. They tell a sinner to believe, not work.

The three comparisons mentioned in Hebrews 8:6 are not the only comparisons in the Book of Hebrews. The whole book is a series of contrasts between the "better things" believers have under the new covenant. John MacArthur has given the best short summary of the heart of the message of Hebrews that I have ever read.

> The epistle to the Hebrews is a study in contrast, between the imperfect and incomplete provisions of the Old Covenant, given under Moses, and the infinitely better provisions of the New Covenant offered by the perfect High-Priest, God's only Son the Messiah, Jesus Christ. Included in the "better" provisions are: a better hope, testament, promise, sacrifice, substance, country, and resurrection. Those who belong 4to the

New Covenant dwell in a completely new and heavenly atmosphere, they worship a heavenly Savior, have a heavenly calling, receive a heavenly gift, are citizens of a heavenly country, look forward to a heavenly Jerusalem, and have their names written in heaven.

One of the key theology themes in Hebrews is that all believers now have direct access to God under the New Covenant and, therefore may approach the throne of God boldly (4:16; 10:22). One's hope is in the very presence of God, into which he follows the Savior 6:19; 10:19, 20). The primary teaching symbolized by the tabernacle service was that believers under the covenant of law did not have direct access to the presence of God (9:8), but were shut out of the Most Holy Place. The Book of Hebrews may briefly be summarized in this way: Believers in Jesus Christ, as God's perfect sacrifice for sin, have the perfect High Priest through whose ministry everything is new and better than under the covenant of law. [34]

MacArthur's statement, with which I totally agree, "The primary teaching symbolized by the tabernacle service was that believers under the covenant of law did not have direct access to the presence of God (9:8), but were shut out of the Holy of Holies," is in total disagreement with the Westminster Confession. Covenant theology's view of continuity/discontinuity necessitates that Israel had all of the blessings that the Church has but not to the same degree.

The liberty which Christ hath purchased for believers under the gospel consists in their freedom from the guilt of sin, the condemning wrath of God, the curse of the moral law; and in their being delivered from this present evil world, bondage to Satan, and dominion of sin, from the evil of afflictions, the sting of death, the victory of the grave, and everlasting damnation; as also in their free access to God, and their yielding obedience unto him, not out of slavish fear, but a child-like love

---

[34] John MacArthur, *Hebrews Macarthur Bible Studies*, (Nashville, TN: Thomas Nelson, 2007), 3

and willing mind. All which were common also to believers under the law; but under the New Testament the liberty of Christians is further enlarged in their freedom from the yoke of the ceremonial law, to which the Jewish Church was subjected; and in greater boldness of access to the throne of grace, and in fuller communications of the free Spirit of God, than believers under the law did ordinarily partake of.[35]

The first half of that statement listing the blessings of believers living under the gospel is an excellent summary. It sounds like these blessing are unique to new covenant believers; however, the confession then upends everything it has just stated. "All which were common also to believers under the law." To say that new covenant believers "had greater boldness of access to the throne of grace" is like saying the veil was *partially* closed under the old covenant and *more opened* under the new covenant Scripture is explicit in stating that the veil totally closed off entrance into the Most Holy place. To speak of an old covenant believer having *any* "boldness of access to the throne of grace "is to add to Scripture. I am sure the framers of the Westminster Confession never intended to minimize the glory of the new covenant, but they could not have done so any better if they had deliberately tried! In chapter 6 we will look at the rending of the veil the day our Lord cried, "It is finished." We will see, among other things, just how wrong the *Westminster Confession* is on "access into the Most Holy Place."

---

[35] *Westminster Confession* - Chapter XX, Of Christian Liberty, and Liberty of Conscience

Theology of the Veil
Chapter 6

In chapter 5 we compared a statement by John MacArthur with a statement from the Westminster Confession of Faith on the same subject. Let me repeat part of each quotation.

> One of the key theological themes in Hebrews is that all believers now have direct access to God under the New Covenant and, therefore may approach the throne of God boldly (4:16; 10:22) ... believers under the covenant of law did not have direct access to the presence of God (9:8), but were shut out of the Holy of Holies.

Compare that statement with the following statement from the *Westminster Confession of Faith.*

> The liberty which Christ hath purchased for believers under the gospel consists in their freedom from the guilt of sin, the condemning wrath of God, the curse of the moral law; and in their being delivered from this present evil world, bondage to Satan, and dominion of sin, from the evil of afflictions, the sting of death, the victory of the grave, and everlasting damnation; as also in their free access to God, and their yielding obedience unto him, not out of slavish fear, but a child-like love and willing mind. All which were common also to believers under the law; ...

The first half of the statement in the *Westminster Confession of Faith* listing the blessings of believers "living under the gospel" is an excellent and accurate summary of what the New Testament teaches. It sounds like all of these blessings are unique to new covenant "believers living under the gospel," however, that is not what the Confession means. The Confession then upends everything it has just stated by insisting "All which were common also to believers under the law." The

Confession is insisting that old and new covenant believers both have all of the same blessings including "free access to God". Not only is there not a stitch of textual evidence for that statement, the statement clearly contradicts Paul's theology of new covenant access to God in Ephesians and Hebrews. That statement is one of what Covenant Theology calls "a good and necessary consequence." The "one covenant with two administrations" advocated by Covenant Theology is essential to that system of Theology. The old covenant and new covenant cannot actually be different covenants in that system. They must be the same covenant in nature and substance and are merely two administrations of that one and same covenant. What the Bible calls the "old covenant," Covenant Theology calls "the older covenant of grace" and what the Bible calls, "the new covenant," Covenant Theology calls "the newer covenant of grace." The Bible specifically uses the words "old and new covenant" and never once refers to a new and old "administration" of the same covenant. This forces that theology to insist that Israel had every spiritual blessing, including "free access to God," or entrance into the Most Holy Place, that the Church enjoys today. This contradicts everything the veil in the Tabernacle separating the Holy Place from the Most Holy Place was meant to teach.

Direct access into the presence of God, the heavenly Most Holy Place, is a New Testament doctrine. The Book of Ephesians and the Book of Hebrews make that very clear. Look at three New Testament passages that speak of the new and total access into God's presence that new covenant believers have but old covenant believers did not have. We not only have a total and permanent peace with God, we have a free access into the heavenly Most Holy Place that old covenant believers did not have. You cannot understand the meaning and purpose of the veil in the Tabernacle and at the same time insist that old covenant believers had access inside that veil.

We will come back to the theology of the veil. That subject is vital in understanding the priestly work of Christ.

First passage:

> *Therefore, since we have been justified through faith, we have peace with God through our Lord Jesus Christ, through whom we have gained access by faith into this grace in which we now stand. And we rejoice in the hope of the glory of God* (Rom. 5:1, 2).

The "access" into the presence of God, the Most Holy Place, described in these verses is a blessing peculiar to the new covenant believers. This blessing is in contrast to the old covenant believer being shut out of the Most Holy Place. This is described in Exodus and Leviticus. The old covenant message of "stay away upon pain of death" has been replaced with the new covenant message of "come and welcome." The message given under the old covenant (Lev. 16:1, 2) was both clear and emphatic. No one except Aaron was allowed access into the Most Holy Place and, he was only allowed to enter on one day of the year, the Day of Atonement. The radically different message under the new covenant is just as clear and emphatic. It says:

> *Therefore, brothers, since we have confidence to enter the Most Holy Place by the blood of Jesus, by a new and living way opened for us through the curtain, that is, his body, and since we have a great priest over the house of God, let us draw near to God with a sincere heart in full assurance of faith, having our hearts sprinkled to cleanse us from a guilty conscience and having our bodies washed with pure water* (Heb. 10:19-22).

What an amazing difference between the old covenant message of "stay away" and the "come boldly" message of the new covenant. Our boldness to come into the Most Holy Place (Rom. 5:1, 2) is based on our assurance that Christ, in his atoning death, has forever "abolished in his flesh the enmity, even the law of commandments."

Second passage:

by abolishing in his flesh the law with its commandments and reg-
ulations. His purpose was to create in himself one new man out of the
two, thus making peace, and in this one body to reconcile both of them
to God through the cross, by which he put to death their hostility. He
came and preached peace to you who were far away and peace to those
who were near. For through him we both have access to the Father by
one Spirit (Eph. 2:15-18).

The shed blood of Christ "abolished in his flesh" (his sinless human nature) the enmity (wrath) of the law of God
against us. The free access that new covenant believes have
into God's presence is possible only because the Tables of the
Covenant in the Ark of the Covenant (the Ten Commandments) have been done away in Christ. The peace preached
in the new covenant is possible because the enmity against us
as lawbreakers has been born by Christ on the cross. This
peace is now preached to the Jew as the true gospel, and the
same Gospel is preached to the Gentiles, those who were
"afar off."

We should mention that you can reconcile enemies but you
cannot reconcile enmity. Enmity must be removed before
there can be true reconciliation. The enmity of God against us
was removed by our blessed substitute on the cross. He was
"made to be sin for us" (2 Cor. 5:23) for us. The enmity in us
against God (Rom. 8:7 NKJV) was removed by the Holy Spirit
in regeneration. He took out our stony hearts that hated God
and his authority and gave us a heart of flesh upon which was
written the Law of Christ. Robed in the righteousness of
Christ we now have boldness and access with confidence to
enter the Most Holy Place. I repeat, I agree with John MacArthur that this is a new covenant blessing the old covenant believer did not have.

Third passage:

In whom we have boldness and access with confidence by the faith
of him (Eph. 3:12 KJV).

The boldness and confidence to enter the very place an old covenant believer was forbidden to enter upon pain of death is the liberty of conscience that enables us to say, "Abba, Father." The old covenant believer thought of God primarily as the "covenant God" and not as "Father." Jesus taught the new covenant believer to think and pray in terms of "our Father." For an excellent development of this fact see Chapter 19, "Sons of God" in J.I. Packer's excellent book, *Knowing God*. [36]

There are two biblical facts that must be understood. (1) The new covenant believer's conscience is "not under law" (Rom. 6:14) in a way that an old covenant believer's conscience could never be, and (2) an old covenant believer's conscience was "under the law" in a way a new covenant believer must never allow his conscience to be. A new covenant believer can sing, "He has hushed the Law's loud thunder, he has brought us near to God." You cannot be "under the law" without hearing its thunder. It is freedom from the law in the conscience that gives freedom of access into the heavenly Most Holy Place. That is what it means to "come boldly to the throne of grace without fear." An old covenant believer had to wait until the coming of Christ to fulfill the promise made to the Fathers before he could sing "the terrors of law, with me have nothing to do. My Savior's obedience and blood hide all my transgressions from view." Understanding the access to God given to us by the atoning work of Christ begins with understanding the hanging of the veil in Exodus 40:21 and the rending of that same veil in Mathew 27:51. Scofield has an interesting footnote on Exodus 26:31.

The inner veil, type of Christ's human body (Matt. 26:26; 27:50; Heb. 10:20). This veil, barring entrance into the holiest, was the most expressive symbol of the truth that "by the deeds of the law shall no flesh be justified" (Rom. 3:20, Heb. 9:8). Rent

---

[36] (Downers Grove, IL: InterVarsity Press, 1973)

by an unseen hand when Christ died (Matt. 27:51) thus giving instant access to God to all who come by faith in Him, it was the end of all legality; the way to God was open. It is deeply significant that the priests must have patched together again the veil that God had rent, for the temple services went on yet for nearly forty years. That patched veil is Galatianism—the attempt to put saint or sinner back under the law (Cf. Gal. 1:6-9). *Anything* but "the *grace* of Christ" is "another gospel," and under anathema. [37]

In each case when the New Testament first introduced Christ as fulfilling one of the offices of Prophet, Priest, and King, it also accompanied each fulfillment with a miraculous sign. The sign showing Christ fulfilling and replacing the Aaronic priesthood is the rending of the veil recorded in Matthew 27:50, 51. I never realized how important this miraculous sign was until I started to write this book. Let's try to unpack the theology behind the hanging and the rending of veil. The rending of the veil is one the greatest object lessons that God ever gave! Israel's failure to learn the lesson taught in the rending of the veil shows how thick the veil of willful ignorance was that blinded them to the gospel that their Messiah had come (2 Cor. 3:14, 15). We will ask and try to answer some obvious questions. Our key text will be Matthew 27:50, 51.

> *Jesus, when he had cried again with a loud voice, yielded up the ghost. And, behold, the veil of the temple was rent in twain from the top to the bottom ...* (Matt. 27:50, 51a KJV).

First: What veil is Matthew talking about? He mentions it was the "veil of the temple." He is referring to the veil that separated the Holy Place from the most Holy Place in the Tabernacle that God instructed Moses to build.

---

[37] *The First Scofield Reference Bible* (Westwood, NJ: Barbour and Company, 1986), 104.

> *And thou shalt make a vail of blue, and purple, and scarlet, and fine twined linen of cunning work: with cherubims shall it be made* (Ex. 26:31).

Exodus 25-40 records the instructions, and the subsequent carrying out of those instructions that God gave Moses in exactly how to build the Tabernacle.

Second: When was the veil hung in place? The veil was the last thing put in place when the Tabernacle was built. Its hanging is described in Exodus 40.

Third: Why was the veil hung? The veil was an integral part of the Levitical system of worship, and as such, it contributed to the overall purpose of that system of worship. We do not have to guess at what that purpose was. God does not always tell us why he does, or does not, do a certain thing. Preachers and writers often speculate and "fill in" what God choose to leave out. This is especially true in the area of typology. As the Dutchman says, "some weird and wonderful" theology has been peddled by building a doctrine on your idea of what God meant but did not state. In the case of the hanging of the veil, we are specifically told what the purpose of the veil was as a part of the Levitical system of worship, and we are also told what the specific purpose of the veil was in its own right.

Look first at the veil as part of the Levitical system of worship. Hebrews is quite clear about what God was seeking to teach in that old system of worship. In Hebrews 9:1-8, the writer gives a short summary of the ritual on the Day of Atonement. He emphasized the High Priest entering the Most Holy Place with blood and sprinkling the mercy seat. Hebrews 9:8 then tells us what God was teaching in those symbolical actions.

> *The Holy Spirit was showing by this that the way into the Most Holy Place had not yet been disclosed as long as the first tabernacle was still standing* (Heb. 9:8).

Contrary to the *Westminster Confession,* the whole old covenant system of worship was designed to teach that the way into the Most Holy Place was totally off limits prior to the rending of the veil. Let me quote that verse using two other versions.

> *By these things the Holy Spirit means for us to understand that the way to the holy of holies was not yet open, that is, so long as the first tent and all that it stands for still exist.* [38]

> *The Holy Spirit is making clear that the way into the holy place had not yet appeared as long as the old tabernacle was standing* (Heb. 9:8, NET).

I do not want to beat a dead horse, but I find it hard to understand how anyone can believe that the old covenant believer had the same "free access to God" that a new covenant believer has when the Holy Spirit "has made it clear that the way into the holy place" had not yet been opened by the atoning work of Christ. Hebrews 9:8 is clear on the subject.

Exodus 40:21 tells us exactly what the purpose was in hanging the veil. It acted as a shield or protection of the Ark of the Covenant. The veil not only kept the people from entering the Most Holy Place, it also kept God in the Most Holy Place. If an Israelite would have beheld God face to face, that person would have been consumed. The cloud and fire that hovered over the Most Holy Place day and night was proof that God was dwelling among his people. The veil kept them from entering the Most Holy Place and being consumed, and the veil also enabled God to be among his people without consuming them. We will come back to this point and show why this was essential.

---

[38] J.B. Phillips, *The New Testament in Modern English* (New York, NY: Galahad Books, 1972), 466

And he brought the ark into the tabernacle, hung the protecting curtain, and shielded the ark of the testimony from view, just as the Lord had commanded Moses (Ex. 40:21, NET).

Fourth: Scripture makes a special point of establishing exactly when the veil was rent in half. Notice how careful the Holy Spirit is. "At that moment" pinpoints preciously the time of the rending of the veil as immediately, "at that moment," when Christ cried out, "It is finished," and yielded up his spirit to the Father.

And when Jesus had cried out again in a loud voice, he gave up his spirit.

At that moment the curtain of the temple was torn in two from top to bottom. The earth shook and the rocks split (Matt. 27:50, 51).

Fifth: Why was it torn from top to bottom? Probably to show it was the work of God and not man. Since Scripture does not specifically answer this question we qualify this as "probably."

Sixth: What was God teaching by rending the veil, or put another way, what is the theology behind the rending of the veil? God was showing that the old covenant, and everything brought into being by that covenant, was now done away and has been, in each case, replaced by something better under the new covenant.

A short review of the dimensions of the tabernacle would be beneficial. The actual tabernacle was made up of three sections and measured 150' x 75'. Inside the tabernacle was divided into two sections. The larger section was called the Holy Place. It was 30' x 15'. Most of the priestly work was done by the sons of Aaron in this room. The smaller room was called the Most Holy Place. It was 15' square. A veil separated the Holy Place and the Most Holy Place. In the Most Holy Place was the Ark of the Covenant. No one was allowed to enter the Most Holy Place except the High Priest and he could enter, with blood, only on one day a year—the Day of Atonement.

We will begin to understand the ministry of the High Priest by looking at the theology of the veil. What is its primary theological significance? We have already noted the veil separated the Holy Place and the Most Holy Place. The Most Holy Place was the holiest and most sacred spot on earth. The hanging of the veil closing off the Most Holy Place was the finishing act in building the Tabernacle. We read, "So Moses finished the work," and when the veil was hung, the "glory of the Lord" filled the Most Holy Place. This meant that God had entered the Most Holy Place and his immediate presence was seen in a cloud by day and a fire in the cloud by night. God was literally "dwelling among his people."

> Then Moses set up the courtyard around the tabernacle and altar and put up the curtain at the entrance to the courtyard. And so Moses finished the work.
>
> Then the cloud covered the Tent of Meeting, and the glory of the Lord filled the tabernacle. Moses could not enter the Tent of Meeting because the cloud had settled upon it, and the glory of the Lord filled the tabernacle.
>
> In all the travels of the Israelites, whenever the cloud lifted from above the tabernacle, they would set out; but if the cloud did not lift, they did not set out — until the day it lifted. So the cloud of the Lord was over the tabernacle by day, and fire was in the cloud by night, in the sight of all the house of Israel during all their travels (Ex. 40:33-38).

In order to understand the meaning and importance of the veil, we cannot start with the veil. The veil itself was not holy. What was holy was what the veil "shielded" (Ex. 40:21). Remember Scripture says the veil "shielded the ark of the covenant." The ark was a box 3.75 feet long, 2.25 feet wide and 2:25 feet high and overlaid within and without with pure gold. The lid of the box was called the "mercy seat" and was made of pure gold. There were two cherubs facing each other with outspread wings and made of pure gold. One cherub was placed at each end of the ark (Ex. 25:10, 11, 17-21). The Ark of the Covenant was designed so it could be picked up and carried without the ark itself ever being touched by human hands. It had four gold rings, one in each corner, and two staves overlaid with gold were put through the rings. The staves were like handles and were left in the ark and never removed. Four men would pick up the ark by the staves and carry the ark without actually touching it (Ex. 25: 12-15).

We need to ask why the Ark of the Covenant was so holy that a special room was built just to house that one piece of furniture and a special veil was hung that acted as a shield for it. The ark was not allowed to even be touched upon pain of death. The primary reason that the Ark of the Covenant, or as it is often called in Scripture, the Ark of the Testimony, is so holy is clearly stated in Scripture. Exodus 25:22 states the mercy seat, or lid of the ark, was the one and only place that God would meet with his people. The Most Holy Place in the Tabernacle was the dwelling place of God among his people. When the lid of the Ark of the Covenant, the mercy seat, was sprinkled with blood, God would meet with Aaron as the people's representative. We will come back to this point when we look at Aaron's work on the Day of Atonement. The new covenant mercy seat is a type of the cross. That is the only place that God will meet the sinner.

> *There, above the cover between the two cherubim that are over the ark of the Testimony, I will meet with you and give you all my commands for the Israelites* (Ex. 25:22).

Very few commentators emphasize the fact that the explicit message of the religion of the old covenant was not "come and welcome." It was "God is holy; you are a sinner, stay away." It is true that the sacrificial system, feasts and rituals offered ceremonial cleansing that temporally "covered sin" and gave a promise of a future redeemer who would solve the sin problem by actually paying its debt, but there was nothing in the whole Mosaic religion that could give the conscience assurance to enter the Most Holy Place behind the veil. That must wait until the "time of reformation." That must wait for a religion based on sovereign grace brought into being by the once for all sufficient sacrifice of our new covenant great High Priest, the Lord Jesus Christ.

The old covenant religion was based on a just, holy, good law. Its function and purpose was to close man's mouth in shame and make him admit his guilt. The old covenant believer had a hope in a coming Messiah but only the actual coming of the Messiah could fulfill hope. The Messiah would fulfill and replace the old covenant with a new and better covenant. The new covenant believer has a better hope but that hope also awaits a future fulfillment when faith gives way to sight at the second coming.

Hebrews 9 is a summary of what we have been saying. An understanding of the writer's argument in this chapter will answer a lot of theological questions.

1 *Then verily the first covenant had also ordinances of divine service, and a worldly sanctuary.* [Don't confuse the covenant with the "ordinances of divine services" that were essential to administer the covenant.]

2 *For there was a tabernacle made; the first, wherein was the candlestick, and the table, and the shewbread; which is called the sanctuary.*

3 *And after the second veil, the tabernacle which is called the Holiest of all;*

4 *Which had the golden censer, and the ark of the covenant overlaid round about with gold, wherein was the golden pot that had manna, and Aaron's rod that budded, and the tables of the covenant;*

5 *And over it the cherubims of glory shadowing the mercyseat; of which we cannot now speak particularly.*

6 *Now when these things were thus ordained, the priests went always into the first tabernacle, accomplishing the service of God.*

7 *But into the second went the high priest alone once every year, not without blood, which he offered for himself, and for the errors of the people:*

8 *The Holy Ghost this signifying, that the way into the holiest of all was not yet made manifest, while as the first tabernacle was yet standing:* [The Tabernacle building stood until 70 AD. The Tabernacle system of worship ended with the rending of the veil. Judaism was God's ordained religion. However, when our Lord ratified the New Covenant with his atoning blood, the Old Covenant system of religion was no longer God's religion. It was now just an empty shell. What was once God's revealed religion has now become only "the Jew's religion" (Gal. 1:14). Any animal sacrifices offered after the rending of the veil was done in open rebellion to God's revelation.]

9 *Which was a figure for the time then present, in which were offered both gifts and sacrifices, that could not make him that did the service perfect, as pertaining to the conscience;* [The sacrificial system could "cover" sin for one year but it could not make atonement, actually pay for sin and "cleanse the conscience." The conscience cannot not be satisfied until we are sure that God is satisfied, and nothing but the blood and righteousness of Christ will satisfy God's holy character and covenant.]

10 *Which stood only in meats and drinks, and divers washings, and carnal ordinances, imposed on them until the time of reformation.*

11 *But Christ being come an high priest of good things to come, by a greater and more perfect tabernacle, not made with hands, that is to say, not of this building;*

12 *Neither by the blood of goats and calves, but by his own blood he entered in once into the holy place, having obtained eternal redemption for us.*

13 *For if the blood of bulls and of goats, and the ashes of an heifer sprinkling the unclean, sanctifieth to the purifying of the flesh:*

14 *How much more shall the blood of Christ, who through the eternal Spirit offered himself without spot to God, purge your conscience* [Satisfying the conscience is essential to a valid assurance of eternal security in Christ. This is impossible as long as the conscience is under the Old Covenant." Nothing in the Old Covenant could satisfy conscience] *from dead works to serve the living God?*

15 *And for this cause* [to effect the purging of the conscience] *he is the mediator of the new testament* [the better covenant], *that by means of death, for the redemption of the transgressions that were under the first testament, they which are called might receive the promise of eternal inheritance* (KJV).

In the following chapter we will look at the Day of Atonement as set forth in Leviticus 16. All agree that this chapter is setting forth the gospel in typology. Aaron was a clear type of Christ. Several things are important when emphasizing that Aaron's ministry could not accomplish a real atonement for sin. Aaron and his ministry, along with the old covenant upon which it was based, had to be replaced. This does not mean that Aaron's ministry was in any way wrong or defective or that Aaron was not faithful in doing what God told him to do. Replacing an old covenant with a new and better covenant is in no sense replacing a "bad" covenant with a "good" covenant. The old covenant and Aaron's ministry totally fulfilled the purpose for which God gave it. Nothing in the old covenant was ever intended to satisfy either God's holy character or the sinner's conscience. The covenant and all of Aaron's work was perfectly successful in fulfilling God's intended purpose. It accomplished exactly what God deigned and purposed it to do. It was designed to convince the sinner that he was totally shutout from God because of his sin. The veil could not possibly show that fact any more clearly. The old covenant was a "killing covenant" that administered death.

In order for a Jew to be saved under the new covenant, he would have to give up nearly everything in his religion. The priest, the covenant, the sacrifices, the holy days and feasts, etc. were all gone and everything was now based on faith instead of sight. Aaron, the Israelite's high priest, was visible in his work. The sinner could see Aaron go into the Most Holy Place with the lamb's blood in a basin. He would look in awe at the beautiful special robes that Aaron only wore on the Day of Atonement. The sinner could see the cloud and fire in the cloud that assured him of God's presence in the camp.

All of that is gone with the coming of the Messiah. The true high priest has ascended into heaven and we no longer see him visibly. We have his promise that he will return and take us to heaven, but in the mean time we face difficult times. It is only as we believe God's promise that we can have hope in this present evil age. The Book of Hebrews assures the Jewish Christian that he has gained more than he lost in losing everything in the old covenant; he has gained, in Christ, more than he lost in Adam. He had to give up his special covenant, his priest, the whole sacrificial system, his special national privileges and many other things, but in every instance he received something better. He lost Aaron and gained Christ. He lost an altar and a sacrificial lamb and gained the cross and the true Lamb of God. John MacArthur has stated this clearly.

> The epistle to the Hebrews is a study in contrast, between the imperfect and incomplete provisions of the Old Covenant, given under Moses, and the infinitely better provisions of the New Covenant offered by the perfect High Priest, God's only Son, and the Messiah, Jesus Christ. Included in the "better" provisions are: a better hope, testament, promise, sacrifice, substance, country and resurrection. Those who belong to the New Covenant dwell in a completely new and heavenly atmosphere, they worship a heavenly Savior, have a heavenly calling, receive a heavenly gift, are citizens of a heavenly country,

look forward to a heavenly Jerusalem, and have their names written in heaven.[39]

We will, like an Israelite, only grasp the wonder and glory of the new covenant as we see how that New Covenant surpasses the glory of the old covenant. The Jew could not move into the new covenant until he left the old covenant and all it brought into being. We must not try to Judaize Christianity by putting the Christian's conscience under the law, and likewise, we must not try to Christianize the old covenant by reading distinctly new covenant blessings like the free access into God's presence back to the old covenant experience. The rending of the veil was essential before there was access into God's presence.

A Christian lawyer was witnessing to a young student. The boy said, "I could never become a Christian because you have to give up so much." The lawyer asked the boy if he had any nickels in his pocket. The boy asked the man why he wanted to know if he had any nickels. The lawyer said, "I will give you a half a dollar for each nickel you have." He boy went through his pockets carefully. After looking in vain for a nickel he said, "I have two dimes and a quarter." The lawyer said, "Would you give me a nickel for this half a dollar if you had a nickel?" The boy said, "I would be a fool not to trade a nickel for a half dollar." The lawyer said, "But you would have to give up your nickel." The boy said, "But look what I would be getting in its place." Many Jews, and some theologians, want to hold on to the nickels of the old covenant and miss the half dollars of new covenant.

---

[39] MacArthur, *Hebrews*, 3

Christ, Our Atonement
Chapter 7

The yearly Day of Atonement, as recorded in Leviticus 16, was the most important day on Israel's calendar. It was the one day every year that Aaron, the High Priest, was allowed to go behind the veil and enter the Most Holy Place. This day Aaron went into the Most Holy Place and sprinkled the mercy seat with blood. This ritual covered Israel's sin for a year. There is not a type of Christ's atoning work in the Old Testament Scriptures that sets forth the cross work of Christ as clearly as Aaron's work on the Day of Atonement. On that day Aaron not only performed the two major functions of a priest: (1) to offer a sacrifice and (2) to make intercession, but he performed both of these things behind the veil in the Most Holy Place. Aaron presented the blood from the goat that had been sacrificed, sprinkled it on the mercy seat of the Ark in the Most Holy Place and pleaded for Israel's forgiveness. Leviticus 16 shows the atonement of Christ in typology. Here is God's instruction on how the Day of Atonement was to be observed.

The instructions begin with a warning. No one except Aaron is allowed to enter the Most Holy Place, and he is to enter only on the Day of Atonement. God reminds Aaron in verse 1 of the death of his two sons, Nadab and Abiuh, (see Lev. 10:1-3) when they "offered unauthorized fire" before the Lord.

The Lord spoke to Moses after the death of the two sons of Aaron who died when they approached the Lord (Lev. 16:1).

Aaron is specifically warned that he will die like his two sons if he comes into the Most Holy Place at any time other than the Day of Atonement.

> *The Lord said to Moses: "Tell your brother Aaron not to come whenever he chooses into the Most Holy Place behind the curtain in front of the atonement cover on the ark, or else he will die, because I appear in the cloud over the atonement cover"* (Lev.6:2).

Aaron is then instructed exactly how he is to approach God in the Most Holy Place. He first brings a sin offering and a burnt offering. He then fully bathes and puts on plain linen clothing including his underwear. These are special garments that Aaron will only wear on the Day of Atonement. The rest of the year he wears the clothes described in Exodus 28:3-35. His regular clothes were very ornate and colorful. On the Day of Atonement Aaron will lay aside his regular ornate high priestly clothes, bathe himself and put on the special plain linen clothing. He will put the special linen clothes on when he first comes into the Most Holy Place, and he will take them off after the scapegoat is released and will not wear them again for another year.

The laying aside of the royal clothes and putting on the plain clothing reminds us of the fact that our Lord's atonement was accomplished in his humanity, that is, as "the man Christ Jesus." It was not the Son of God in the full power of his deity that defeated Satan, but it was Jesus, the son of Mary, our true kinsman, our older brother who fought and conquered Satan as our substitute. In his incarnation our Lord did not cease to be absolute deity, but he did lay aside the exercise of his deity and put on the robe of human flesh with all its limitations—yet without sin. He laid aside the use of the splendor and glory of his deity and robed himself in the plain linen of our humanity in order to become one with us in our humanity and function as our kinsman redeemer.

"This is how Aaron is to enter the sanctuary area: with a young bull for a sin offering and a ram for a burnt offering. 4 He is to put on the sacred linen tunic, with linen undergarments next to his body; he is to tie the linen sash around him and put on the linen turban. These are sacred garments; so he must bathe himself with water before he puts them on" (Lev.16:3-4).

Aaron then takes two goats from the congregation for a sin offering and one ram for a burnt offering. He offers the bullock for himself and his house. Everything that in any way involves either the priest or the people must be the cleanest by sprinkled blood because it has been defiled by contact with sin.

"From the Israelite community he is to take two male goats for a sin offering and a ram for a burnt offering.

Aaron is to offer the bull for his own sin offering to make atonement for himself and his household" (Lev.16:5-6).

The symbolism of the two goats is the heart of the Day of Atonement. Two goats are chosen from among the congregation. The High Priest then cast lots and designate the one goat as "the Lord's goat." This goat will be slain and its blood sprinkled on the mercy seat in the Most Holy Place. This goat illustrates the truth of the propitiatory work on the cross. The NIV states the essence of its meaning:

God presented him as a sacrifice of atonement, through faith in his blood. He did this to demonstrate his justice, because in his forbearance he had left the sins committed beforehand unpunished—he did it to demonstrate his justice at the present time, so as to be just and the one who justifies those who have faith in Jesus (Rom. 3:25-26).

The mercy seat is the place of the propitiation or a sacrifice of atonement. It is the aspect of Christ's sacrifice that pays for sin and satisfies the holy character of God. There is no word hated as deeply by liberal churchmen as the word *propitiation*. The idea that a God of love could have a wrath that needed to be satisfied with a sacrifice is a monstrous idea to a liberal.

They insist that the suffering caused by sin is not because there is wrath in God but only because the nature of sin carries suffering as a consequence. Wrath is like the heat in a radiator. If you touch a hot radiator you will feel pain, but that is not because there is wrath in the radiator. The liberal's problem is his misunderstanding of the true nature of God. He begins with love instead of beginning with holiness. The death of the "Lord's goat" shows the necessity of a death to pay for sin. I used to say, "God owes no man anything," but I was wrong. God owes every sinner the wages of sin, namely death as the penalty for sin. God is honest and will pay the earned wages.

After sprinkling the mercy seat with blood, Aaron will put both hands on the second goat and confess the sins of Israel. This illustrates the doctrine of imputation. The people's sins are symbolically imputed, "put on," the goat and the goat is taken out into the wilderness and forever lost. The work of the second goat illustrates the doctrine of expiation of sin by our Lord. He not only paid for sin, but he literally carried the sin away. He bore the penalty of our sin on the cross and then buried it forever in his tomb. He went into the grave with our sin on him and left the sin behind when he arose from death. The Holy Ghost uses some strong metaphors to illustrate this truth.

One of the metaphors is Micah 7:19: "You will again have compassion on us; you will tread our sins underfoot and hurl all our iniquities into the depths of the sea." A young Christian was on a cruise ship and started to flip a silver dollar into the air. Each time he flipped it a little higher. When a small crowd gathered, the young man flipped the coin very high, and the wind took it into the ocean. The young man asked the crowd, "How many of you believe we could turn around and find that coin?" Everyone smiled and some said, "No way. It is gone forever." The young man said, "I think you are right.

There is something else that is buried in the depth of the sea and will never be found, and that it is my sin." He then proceeded with presenting the gospel.

One of my favorite passages that teach this truth is Psalm 103:12: "as far as the east is from the west, so far has he removed our transgressions from us." I remember using this text in a sermon. I emphasized that east and west never meet. If you took off in an airplane and flew directly west, you would fly forever and never be flying east. You would always be flying west. If you turned around and flew east, you would fly forever without ever flying west. As I said, east and west never meet. The same thing is not true if you fly either north or south. If you fly south, you will start flying north when you cross the South Pole, or if you fly north, you will start flying south when you cross the North Pole. After the service ended an elderly lady smiled and said, "I am sure glad the Holy Ghost knows the difference between east and west and north and south." From north to south is not very far but from east to west is beyond measuring.

> *Then he is to take the two goats and present them before the Lord at the entrance to the Tent of Meeting. He is to cast lots for the two goats—one lot for the Lord and the other for the scapegoat. Aaron shall bring the goat whose lot falls to the Lord and sacrifice it for a sin offering. But the goat chosen by lot as the scapegoat shall be presented alive before the Lord to be used for making atonement by sending it into the desert as a scapegoat* (Lev. 16:7-10).

Sin has now both been paid for, carried away and forgotten forever. Aaron slays the bullock to atone for himself and his house. He takes a censer full of hot coals from the altar and sweet incense and goes behind the veil. He pours the incense over the hot coals, and a sweet aroma fills the Most Holy Place.

> *"Aaron shall bring the bull for his own sin offering to make atonement for himself and his household, and he is to slaughter the bull for*

his own sin offering. He is to take a censer full of burning coals from the altar before the Lord and two handfuls of finely ground fragrant incense and take them behind the curtain. He is to put the incense on the fire before the Lord, and the smoke of the incense will conceal the atonement cover above the Testimony, so that he will not die" (Lev.16:11-13).

This is a picture of justification. Aaron stands accepted in the very place that is off-limits upon pain of death for 364 days of the year. He stands in the presence of God as the people's representative, and the sweet smell of the incense fills the room signifying that God is pleased. This acceptance is because of the blood atonement that was made on the coals of fire Aaron is carrying. The Most Holy Place becomes a place of meeting with God in assurance of forgiveness of sins instead of a place of fear and judgment. The Apostle Paul uses the sweet smelling savor image in Ephesians.

. . . . . and live a life of love, just as Christ loved us and gave himself up for us as a fragrant offering and sacrifice to God (Eph. 5:2).

The cross provides an acceptable atonement and changes the smell of death into the smell of grace and forgiveness. All of the ugliness and smell of an animal being sacrificed on hot coals is transformed into the God ordained means of satisfying his perfect holiness. When God sees the blood applied, he sees the perfect obedient sacrifice of his son, and he is well pleased. There is surely nothing "sweet smelling" in the agony of the cross from a human point of view, but God saw the cross as the height of our Lord's obedience. Our Lord was never more pleasing to his father than he was the moment he cried out, "My God, my God, why hast thou forsaken me." At that moment Jesus was putting himself into the hands of his Father to be crucified knowing that he would be vindicated and raised from the dead. This was the act of perfect obedience and faith. The Father raised him from the dead and gave him all power and authority as a reward for his work. Justification robes us in Christ's perfect righteousness, and we are a sweet smelling savor unto God.

We are reminded of Jacob and his mother fooling Isaac and stealing the first-born blessing. Isaac was getting old and blind. He asked Jacob to go hunting, kill a deer and roast it the way he liked it. Rebekah dressed Jacob in Esau's clothes so he would smell like the fields. She put hair on the back of Jacob's hands and the smooth part of his neck. She prepared two goats and made them taste like venison (that was quite a trick!). Isaac was skeptical at first and wanted to feel his son. The hair Rebekah put on Jacob's hands and neck fooled Isaac. Isaac then told Jacob to come near and kiss him. When Isaac kissed Jacob he said, "You smell like Esau," and Isaac blessed Jacob. The whole story is found in Genesis 27.

What a glorious picture of our drawing near to God "in the name of Jesus" and receiving a blessing we did not earn or in any way deserve; however, we did not fool or deceive God. He is fully aware we are trading on the merits of his Son. We come into his presence in the name of Christ because the Father has told us to come trusting in the merits of Christ. When we are washed in the blood of Christ and robed in his righteousness, we "smell like Jesus" and God blesses us "for Jesus sake." He draws us to himself and gives us the kiss of reconciliation.

Leviticus states a truth that needs a constant repetition:

> No one is to be in the Tent of Meeting from the time Aaron goes in to make atonement in the Most Holy Place until he comes out,
> …(Lev. 16:17).

Our Lord performed the work of atonement all by himself. There is no "his part" combined with "our part" in the scheme of grace. When I hear so-called evangelists say, "God has done his part, now you must do your part," I want to shout,

"My part was to run as fast as I could to get away from God, and his part was to run faster and overcome all my resistance." I love the way the writer of Hebrews repeats this same truth:

> *The Son is the radiance of God's glory and the exact representation of his being, sustaining all things by his powerful word. After he had provided purification for sins, he sat down at the right hand of the Majesty in heaven* (Heb. 1:3).

There were no chairs in the tabernacle because the priest's work was never finished. When our Lord, all by himself with no help from us, had "purged our sins," he sat down because his work of atonement was finished. However, he did not sit down on a chair; he sat down on a throne in heaven beside his father. There will never be another Day of Atonement.

There is a lot of confusion concerning the status of an old covenant believer. A lot of the confusion is created by theologians totally misunderstanding the radical difference between the old and new covenants. old covenant believers had a hope in a coming Messiah and were just as "saved by grace" as we are today. They were just as eternally secure in their faith as a believer is today; however, they had no way of knowing they were secure. An old covenant believer would have assurance running out his ears on the Day of Atonement when he saw Aaron coming out of the Most Holy Place. He would know he was safe and secure for a whole year. He would not have known what it was to be united to Christ in his death, burial, resurrection and ascension and be eternally secure in Christ.

There was no sacrifice, including the goat on the Day of Atonement, which would allow an Old Testament believer into the presence of God behind the veil. He could not have had an awareness of eternal security but only an awareness of one year's atonement. He was secure but had no way of knowing it. An old covenant believer, including David, believed his salvation was up for grabs on the Day of Atonement. Some theologians give the impression that old covenant believers chewed gum in disinterest when Aaron went into the Most Holy Place. Such is not the case. The individual believer would have felt his hope of acceptance with God was tied with Aaron's offering being accepted. He did not say or think that the ritual on the Day of Atonement had nothing to do with him because he could somehow look forward to the completed revelation of God in Christ and grasp that he was eternally secure.

A new covenant believer knows he is eternally secure in Christ because many new covenant texts teach that truth. He does not feel he must get converted again every time he sins. He can use the new covenant promises like John 5:24 and Romans 8:1 to maintain assurance in spite of sin. An old covenant believer did not have those promises. The extent of his experience was based on the knowledge he could get from the old covenant, and that knowledge did not include being "seated together with Christ in heaven." He had eternal life but believed he only had a one-year atonement, and he believed he could lose that one year's salvation for willful covenant breaking.

We must not read the New Testament experience as being identical to the experience of an old Covenant believer despite the fact an old Covenant believer had many of the same blessings we enjoy today. Abraham is the prototype for justification for all believers in every dispensation, but that does not mean that Abraham understood and believed Romans 5:1-5. Experience cannot exceed revelation. An old covenant believer did not have the Book of Ephesians and the Book of Romans. He could not see himself "seated in heavenly places in Christ Jesus" since Christ had not yet even died. David was just as eternally secure, despite his sin, as a believer is today, but he believed he could lose his salvation. Psalm 51 is not merely pleading to not lose the assurance of salvation, but it is pleading to not lose salvation. I repeat, David was just as secure as you and me, but he had no revelation upon which to garner assurance of that security. The old covenant believer "hoped" for many things that had to await the coming of the Messiah to fulfill the new covenant. Blessings rooted in the new covenant cannot be experienced until the new covenant is in force. Remember the old covenant believer did not live under the covenant that Christ established; he lived under the law covenant that God established through Moses at Sinai. The new covenant believer is "under grace" in a way an old covenant believer never could be, and the old covenant believer was under law in a way a new covenant believer must never be.

Hebrews 9 gives a review of the Tabernacle ministry on the Day of Atonement. Verse 15 reveals that the New Testament, or covenant, had to be in place before believers could receive the "promise of an eternal inheritance." The one year "covering" of sin on the Day of Atonement was not a real atonement because it was only a temporary promise of a coming atonement. The Day of Atonement was like an "I owe you" that guaranteed a future true atonement. There was no real atonement that could cleanse the conscience until Christ died on the cross. The entire Levitical system was only a type, a foreshadowing. All of the animal sacrifices put together could not actually forgive one sin.

In the next chapter we will look at the theology behind "the testimony" in the ark. A failure to see that the Ten Commandments, or "Tables of the Covenant," is a covenant document and not the so-called "moral law" obscures the biblical meaning of the Day of Atonement.

Ark of the Covenant
Chapter 8

The Day of Atonement must have been an awesome experience for Aaron the High Priest. His heart must have beaten a mile a minute as he pulled the veil back and entered the forbidden Most Holy Place. His finger probably shook as he sprinkled the blood on the mercy seat seven times. Some numbers used in Scripture have great significance.

The number seven seems to represent perfection, and is the sign of God, divine worship, completions, obedience, and rest. The "prince" of Bible numbers, it is used 562 times, including its derivatives (e.g., seventh, sevens). (See Genesis 2:1–4, Psalm 119:164, and Exodus 20:8–11 for just a few examples.)

The number seven is also the most common in biblical prophecy, occurring forty-two times in Daniel and Revelation alone. In Revelation there are seven churches, seven spirits, seven golden candlesticks, seven stars, seven lamps, seven seals, seven horns, seven eyes, seven angels, seven trumpets, seven thunders, seven thousand slain in a great earthquake, seven heads, seven crowns, seven last plagues, seven golden vials, seven mountains, and seven kings.

The sprinkling of blood seven times shows the perfection and completion of Aaron's work. Just as no one assisted him in his work of atonement, no one added anything in any way to that work. The atonement was a work of God alone. The sprinkling of the blood on the mercy seat was a clear picture of Christ presenting himself to the Father in sacrifice. Our Lord was the true propitiatory sacrifice that fulfilled and ended the whole sacrificial system. There will not only never be another Day of Atonement, but there will never be any kind of a blood sacrifice. The entire old covenant is forever done away. At Calvary our blessed substitute shed human but sinless blood and fully paid the debt we owed. The hymn writer had it right, "I owed a debt I could not pay. He paid a debt he did not owe."

The full message of the blood being sprinkled on the mercy seat cannot be understood until we understand the great significance of the Ark of the Covenant. The whole system of atonement centered on the box, or ark, with the solid gold lid called the mercy seat. It is essential that we ask, "What made that box so important?" If you have never studied the biblical answer to that question, I would encourage you read *Tablets of Stone and the History of Redemption*. This is one of the first books I wrote, and it lays a foundation for the theology of law and grace.

One of the reasons the Ark of the Covenant1 was so important was because of what was in it. The ark was built for the distinct purpose of housing the Ten Commandments written on the two stone tablets of the covenant. We must also ask why the Ten Commandments were so important that a special box was built to store the tablets upon which those commandments were inscribed. A box, we might add, that was built with rings and staves to pick it up because God forbid anyone from even touching the actual ark. On one occasion they were moving the ark on a cart and the oxen stumbled. A man named Uzzah put his hand on the ark to steady it, and God killed him on the spot.

> When they came to the threshing floor of Nakon, Uzzah reached out and took hold of the ark of God, because the oxen stumbled. The Lord's anger burned against Uzzah because of his irreverent act; therefore God struck him down, and he died there beside the ark of God (2 Sam. 6:6-7).

Nearly everyone, including me, agrees that the Ark of the Covenant was important because it housed the Ten Commandments. However, it had nothing to do with any idea that the Ten Commandments were the so-called "moral law of God." That idea is a pure theological fantasy without an ounce of biblical evidence. It is a gross misunderstanding of the nature and purpose of the Ten Commandments to think of them as the so-called "moral law." The Ark of the Covenant was holy because the Ten Commandments, or words of the covenant, were written on the Tables of the Covenant in the ark. The Ten Commandments were the summary document of the old covenant that established Israel as a special nation before God. The tablets of the covenant upon which the Ten Commandments were written were to Israel what the Constitution of the United States is to our nation. It is the founding covenant document. To think of the Ten Commandments as the so-called moral law instead of thinking of them as a covenant document is to totally confuse the true importance of those covenant terms written on tables of stone.

The Bible only uses the phrase "Ten Commandments" three times in all of Scripture. All three times are in the Old Testament. The New Testament never uses the words "Ten Commandments." Here is a list of the phrases that the Bible uses as synonyms to describe the Ten Commandments.

Ten Commandments – used 3 times. Never used in New Testament.

Tables of the Testimony – used 2 times. Never used in New Testament.

The Testimony – used 42 times. Never used in the New Testament.

Words of the Covenant – used 4 times. Never used in the New Testament.

Tables of the Covenant – used 4 times. Used once in the New Testament in Hebrews 9:4.

As you can see from this list, the word "testimony" is used more than any other word or phrase as a synonym for the Ten Commandments. You can also see that not a single one of the terms in the list are remotely associated with a so-called "moral law."

The first use of a term in Scripture usually defines the meaning of that term as it will be used in the rest of Scripture. In this case, the first use of the term "Ten Commandments" clearly shows its meaning to be "the words of the covenant."

> *Then the Lord said to Moses, "Write down these words, for in accordance with these words I have made a covenant with you and with Israel." Moses was there with the Lord forty days and forty nights without eating bread or drinking water. And he wrote on the tablets the words of the covenant—the Ten Commandments.*
>
> *When Moses came down from Mount Sinai with the two tablets of the Testimony in his hands, (Ex. 34:27-29a).*

Notice what the Word of God says and also what it does not say. Verse 27 is unmistakably clear, "in acco1dance with these words I have made a covenant with you" can only be referring to the Ten Commandments as the terms of the old covenant. In this text, the Ten Commandments are specifically called the "words of the covenant." Verse 28 is even more specific, "he wrote on the tablets the words of the covenant—the Ten Commandments." It is impossible to more clearly state that the Ten Commandments are the "words of the covenant." Verse 29 calls the Ten Commandments "two tablets of testimony." As noted in the list above, the word "testimony" is used more times in Scripture than all other words or phrases put together to describe the nature of the Ten Commandments. When is the last time you heard the Ten Commandments referred to as the "Testimony" or "Tables of the Testimony?" This word testimony is used so often because the Ten Commandments are the words or terms of the covenant that will furnish the grounds for judging the nation of Israel. They became a nation by entering into a covenant with God on the terms, or words, of the Ten Commandments written on the Tables of the Covenant. They were rejected as a nation on the grounds of habitually breaking those covenant terms. What is missing in these verses is the slightest mention of any idea of the Ten Commandments being the so-called "moral law of God."

The first time I listed these terms that are interchangeable with the Ten Commandments on a chalkboard a young man asked, "Mr. Reisinger, why did you not give any references to the Ten Commandments referring to the moral law?" I replied, "I wish every question I am asked was as easy to answer as that one." The young man was quite surprised when I said, "I did not mention any such verses simply because there are none. The Bible never one time uses the phrase 'moral law' let alone use it as in some way being associated with the Ten Commandments."

The other two places in Scripture that use the term Ten Commandments are just as clear and just as emphatic concerning the identity of the Ten Commandments as Exodus 34:27-29.

> Then the Lord spoke to you out of the fire. You heard the sound of words but saw no form; there was only a voice. He declared to you his covenant, the Ten Commandments, which he commanded you to follow and then wrote them on two stone tablets. (Deut. 4:12-13).

The Holy Spirit wants to be clear that when he is talking about the covenant he is talking about the Ten Commandments, and when he is talking about the Ten Commandments he is talking about "the words of the covenant." The phrase "Ten Commandments" and "words of the covenant" are the same thing. It is impossible to miss the fact that the Bible clearly, consistently and emphatically teaches that the Ten Commandments are the words or summary terms of the old covenant that established Israel as a nation.

> At that time the Lord said to me, "Chisel out two stone tablets like the first ones and come up to me on the mountain. Also make a wooden chest. I will write on the tablets the words that were on the first tablets, which you broke. Then you are to put them in the chest."
>
> So I made the ark out of acacia wood and chiseled out two stone tablets like the first ones, and I went up on the mountain with the two tablets in my hands. The Lord wrote on these tablets what he had written before, the Ten Commandments he had proclaimed to you on the mountain, out of the fire, on the day of the assembly. And the Lord gave them to me. (Deut. 10:1-4).

There is no way that you can make the Ten Commandments to be the so-called "moral law" of God. Covenant theologians insist on making the Ten Commandments to be the so-called moral law instead of being the words or terms of the covenant. They do this without a stitch of textual evidence. They ignore or deny the words just quoted that clearly state the actual "words of the covenant" are the Ten Commandments. This is a classic example of systematic theology interpreting Scripture instead of Scripture texts establishing systematic theology. If Covenant Theology is correct, we should call the ark that houses the Ten Commandments the "ark of the moral law."

Exodus 32-34 records Israel's sin of idolatry while Moses was on the mount receiving the Ten Commandments. When Moses came down from the mount and saw the orgy going on, he smashed the tablets of the testimony, or Ten Commandments, that God had written on the stone tablets. Moses did not smash the first set of the Tablets of the Covenant because they were the so-called moral law, but he smashed them because they were the "the testimony" or summary doctrine of the covenant that established Israel's nationhood. The Holy Spirit calls them the "two tablets of the testimony."

> *Moses turned and went down the mountain with the two tablets of the Testimony in his hands. They were inscribed on both sides, front and back. The tablets were the work of God; the writing was the writing of God, engraved on the tablets* (Ex.32:15-16).

We mentioned earlier that Matthew 27:51 was the key text for any discussion of the rending of the veil. On the cross Jesus cried, "It is finished" and yielded up the ghost. The moment he died the veil in the temple was rent from top to bottom. There is a lot of discussion about what Jesus was referring to when he said, "It is finished." He could have been referring to "the work my Father gave me to do," or he could have meant "my necessary sufferings." Nearly every suggestion fits the context.

One thing that is helpful in understanding the implication of that object lesson and understanding the phrase is seeing the connection between Jesus' statement, "it is finished" and the rending of the veil. The context shows that the rending of the veil was a direct result of Jesus finishing whatever he was talking about. The veil could not be removed until Jesus could say, "It is finished," and once whatever he was talking about was finished the veil was automatically obsolete. "It is finished" and the "rending of the veil" are tied together as essential cause and effect. As long as the old covenant was in effect, the veil must remain in place. The veil shielded the Ark of the Covenant. That veil must remain in place until the terms of the words of the covenant, the Ten Commandments, were fully met and sin was paid for in full.

One thing that was finished was the old covenant. Everything without exception that the old covenant established, the Aaronic priesthood, the sacrificial system, the feast days, the special nation, etc., was totally and permanently finished and replaced with something better. This includes the words of the covenant, the Ten Commandments. Before the better things of the new covenant could be established, the old covenant things had to be perfectly fulfilled and done away with. Our kinsman redeemer was born under the covenant written on the stone Tables of the Covenant in the ark. He perfectly kept all of that covenant's terms and earned the life and righteousness that it promised. He earned every blessing it promised because he kept every precept it demanded. He literally brought to the Tables of the Covenant the holy, sinless and obedient life it demanded. Every precept must be fulfilled. Every term had to be obeyed just as every prophecy had to be fulfilled. Not a jot or tittle could be left unfinished. On the cross our Lord's mind went down through the Old Testament, and he saw one thing in Psalm 69:21 not yet finished ("They put gall in my food and gave me vinegar for my thirst." Psalm 69:21).

> Later, knowing that all was now completed, and so that the Scripture would be fulfilled, Jesus said, "I am thirsty." A jar of wine vinegar was there, so they soaked a sponge in it, put the sponge on a stalk of the hyssop plant, and lifted it to Jesus' lips. When he had received the drink, Jesus said, "It is finished." With that, he bowed his head and gave up his spirit (John 19:28-30).

The moment the last old covenant prophecy was fulfilled, our Lord cried out, "It is finished" and gave up his spirit. The rending of the veil was the evidence that the old was finished and the new had come. Understanding the meaning of this evidence is the beginning of understanding New Covenant Theology.

The last thing put in place when the Tabernacle was built was the veil isolating the Most Holy Place. The Ark of the Covenant was put in place, the Tables of the Covenant, or Ten Commandments, were put in the ark and finally the veil was hung to shield the ark. When the veil was hung, the glory of the Lord filled the Most Holy Place signifying that God had taken up residence in the Most Holy Place. God was truly dwelling "among His people."

The "glory" of God is his immediate presence. The first mention of God's glory is when God appeared on the mountaintop at Sinai. They saw God's glory from a distance. The next time his glory appeared was when the Tabernacle was finished. God had moved into the Most Holy Place, and he was now visibly, day and night, dwelling among his people. In the incarnation, God became flesh and we "beheld his glory." God had moved closer to his people, but he was still hidden to some degree as Wesley wrote in his hymn: "veiled in flesh the Godhead see." On the Day of Pentecost God sent his Holy Spirit to indwell every believer, and God came even closer. Our Lord's prophecy in John 14:17 that the Holy Spirit "was with you and shall be in you" was fulfilled. Some day we shall see him face to face in all his glory.

When the Ark of the Covenant was first placed in the Most Holy Place it contained nothing but the second set of the Tablets of the Covenant. Moses smashed the first set when Israel worshipped the golden calf (Exodus 32). Later two more items were put in the ark. A pot of manna was put in the ark when the children of Israel complained against God for having nothing but manna to eat. This incident is recorded in Numbers 17. The second item put into the ark was the rod that budded when the sons of Korah challenged the authority of Moses and were rebuked by God. This is recorded in Exodus 16:1-34.

These three items in the ark reminded Israel of her sin. When the cherubim looked down on the ark, which signified God looking at the mercy seat, he saw the blood sprinkled; he did not see the emblems of sin in the ark. The sin was covered with the atoning blood. Without the blood, Aaron could not have stood before the mercy seat. The covenant terms, or Ten Commandments, in the ark demanded perfect obedience upon pain of death. As long as the covenant terms in the ark, the Ten Commandments, were in effect, Israel was "under the law" as a covenant of life and death. They were duty bound to obey the covenant terms, the Ten Commandments, written on the Tables of the Covenant in the ark. Once the covenant was broken, the Tables of the Covenant demanded an acceptable sacrifice that would satisfy God's holy character. No son of Adam was ever able to give either of these things to the covenant.

The sacrifice on the Day of Atonement gave a yearly temporary covering, but nothing could actually pay for sin. Neither the people nor Aaron could meet the terms the Tables of the Covenant demanded. They could not bring to the covenant a holy sinless life that earned life and righteousness, nor could they bring an acceptable sacrifice that paid their debt to God and satisfied his holy character. As long as the Tables of the Covenant in the Ark of the Covenant were in effect, Israel's only hope was a future Redeemer. Everything in the religion of Moses was temporary and typical. Its benefits were only for one year.

We need to be reminded that the Day of Atonement was a classic example of the doctrine of limited or particular atonement. There was not a single thing done on that day for the Philistines or any other pagan nation. When Aaron put his hands on the goat and confessed sins, it was Israel's sins alone and not the sins of any pagan nation that he confessed. The blood sprinkled on the mercy seat was to make atonement for Israel not for the Philistines. Aaron had the names of the twelve tribes of Israel on his breast as he applied the blood on the mercy seat. The uniform teaching of both the Old and New Testaments is the coextension of the atoning work and the intercessory work of the High Priest. He prays for those for whom he makes sacrifice. Aaron prayed for those for whom he made sacrifice even as our Lord did the same thing. Jesus said,

> *I pray for them. I am not praying for the world, but for those you have given me, for they are yours* (John 17:9).

I find it impossible to believe that Christ would die for an individual and then not pray for that individual. If we accept the clear teaching of Scripture on the nature of true atonement, we have two choices: 1) Christ died an atoning death for all men, in which case all men without exception will be saved, or 2) Christ died for the sheep the Father gave him, in which case the elect chosen by the Father will be saved.

The type and the anti-type must both teach the same truth. Both Aaron and Christ must teach either a universal or a particular atonement. Everything on Israel's Day of Atonement was particular. Every aspect of Aaron's work involved only the nation of Israel. In John 17: 9 our Lord made it abundantly clear that on God's great Day of Atonement, his son's work was for the elect alone.

Christ, Our Perfect and Compassionate High Priest Chapter 9

Every high priest is selected from among men and is appointed to represent them in matters related to God, to offer gifts and sacrifices for sins. He is able to deal gently with those who are ignorant and are going astray, since he himself is subject to weakness. This is why he has to offer sacrifices for his own sins, as well as for the sins of the people.

No one takes this honor upon himself; he must be called by God, just as Aaron was. So Christ also did not take upon himself the glory of becoming a high priest. But God said to him,

"You are my Son; today I have become your Father" (Heb. 5:1-5).

Chapter 5 begins the longest section in the book of Hebrews and goes all the way through chapter 10, verse 39. The subject of this entire section is the high priestly work of Christ. From both a practical and doctrinal viewpoint, this section is one of the most important in the entire book of Hebrews. It is also one of the most misunderstood passages among sincere Christians. The Roman Catholics and many Anglicans (Episcopalians) grossly ignore or confuse the wonder and glory of Christ's work as high priest by having their leaders assume they are priests capable of being mediators between God and sinners. Arminians falsely assume that the priestly work of Christ is equally on behalf of all men without exception. Most fundamentalists, including the Plymouth Brethren, insist the priestly work of Christ does not begin until his ascension. This limits the high priestly work to intercession, but it is quite clear that the primary work of the high priest in the old covenant was to offer sacrifice. It is just as clear in the New

Testament that Christ's high priestly work includes sacrifice as well as intercession.

The Arminian has no place to put the atoning work of Christ on the cross. All agree it was not his work as prophet or his work as king that made atonement for sin. However, if we put the sacrificial work of the atonement under the office of priest we are well on our way to particular redemption. In order to hold on to universal atonement, the Arminian reduces the priestly work of Christ to be limited to intercession. In this way, Christ's priestly work does not begin until he ascends to heaven and is seated on his throne. However, to hold that view these people must flat out deny the specific words of Christ when he said, "I pray not for the world" (John 17:9). It is abundantly clear that Christ does not act in the place of the non-elect in either his office of prophet or his office of priest. The writer of Hebrews has already mentioned the high priestly work of Christ three times. It is clear from these texts that the priestly work of Christ included reconciliation as well as intercession just as it included both propitiation and expiation.

> For this reason he had to be made like his brothers in every way, in order that he might become a merciful and faithful high priest in service to God, and that he might make atonement for the sins of the people (Heb. 2:17).

> Therefore, holy brothers, who share in the heavenly calling, fix your thoughts on Jesus, the apostle and high priest whom we confess (Heb. 3:1).

> Therefore, since we have a great high priest who has gone through the heavens, Jesus the Son of God, let us hold firmly to the faith we profess. For we do not have a high priest who is unable to sympathize with our weaknesses, but we have one who has been tempted in every way, just as we are—yet was without sin. Let us then approach the throne of grace with confidence, so that we may receive mercy and find grace to help us in our time of need (Heb. 4:14-16).

Our Lord is glorious in both his person and in his work. It is the awesome glory of his person that gives his redemptive work the honor and dignity that it deserves.

...let us note that the Lord Jesus is designed a *"great* High Priest." This word at once emphasizes His excellency and pre-eminency. Never was there, never can there be another, possessed of such dignity and glory. The "greatness" of our High Priest arises, First, from the dignity of His person: He is not only Son of man, but Son of God (Heb. 4:14). Second, from the purity of His nature: He is "without sin" (Heb. 4:15), "holy," (Heb. 7:26). Third, from the eminency of His order: that of Melchizedek (Heb. 5:6). Fourth, from the solemnity of his ordination: "with an oath" (Heb. 7:20, 21)—none other was. Fifth, from the excellency of His sacrifice: "Himself, without spot" (Heb. 9:14). Sixth, from the perfection of His administration (Heb. 7:11, 25)—He has satisfied divine justice, procured Divine favor, given access to the Throne of Grace, secured eternal redemption. Seventh, from the perpetuity of His office: it is untransferable and eternal (Heb. 7:24). From these we may the better perceive the blasphemous arrogance of the Italian pope, who styles himself *"pontifex maximus"*—the *greatest* high priest. [40]

It is interesting to follow biblical arguments and note how logically they are framed. The Holy Spirit knows how to think and how to express the truth. He does not begin his list of comparisons between the old and the new with Moses and Aaron. That would immediately have offended the Jews. The writer starts with angels and talks about a mediator who is holy, acceptable to God, has a heart of compassion for sinners and is just the mediator we need in every way. The writer of Hebrews begins chapter 5 with a description of the high priest's nature and work.

---

[40] Arthur W. Pink, *An Exposition of Hebrews* (Blacksburg, VA: Wilder Publications, 2008), 138.

Every high priest is selected from among men and is appointed to represent them in matters related to God, to offer gifts and sacrifices for sins. He is able to deal gently with those who are ignorant and are going astray, since he himself is subject to weakness. This is why he has to offer sacrifices for his own sins, as well as for the sins of the people.

No one takes this honor upon himself; he must be called by God, just as Aaron was (Heb. 5:1-4).

These verses give a summary of the qualifications of the Levitical high priests. Our Lord fulfilled every one of these qualifications. First of all, the high priest had to be "selected from among men." That means he had to be part of the human family, a true part of Adam's race. An angel could not be a priest, let alone be the high priest. A high priest must partake of the nature of those on whose behalf he acts. He must be a kinsman of those he represents. Second, the high priest did not act as a private individual, but as a public official: "is appointed to represent them." He acted as an appointed representative of sinners. Third, when he approached God he did not come empty handed. He brought "sacrifices … for sins." Fourth, the high priest must realize that he himself was a sinner and needed grace. He had to be able to give hope and comfort to those of his fellow sinners to whom he ministered (verses 2, 3).

Our new covenant high priest was not in any sense a sinner as was Aaron, and part of this particular requirement did not apply to him. The need to be able to sympathize did apply to Christ, and his ability to sympathize with us grew out of his becoming one with us in our humanity. He was tempted in the same way we are tempted, but he never yielded to any temptation. Fifth, he did not presumptuously "decide to be a high priest" by his own choice but was chosen and approved by God (verse 4). Let us look at each of these five things more closely.

The first thing is an emphasis on his humanity. "Every high priest selected from among men…"

An angel would be no fitting priest to act on behalf of men, for he possesses not their nature, is not subject to their temptations, and has no experimental acquaintance with their sufferings; therefore is he unsuited to act on their behalf: therefore is he incapable of having "compassion" upon them, for the motive-spring of all real intercession is heart-felt sympathy. Thus, the primary qualification of a priest is that he must be personally related to, possess the same nature as, those for whose welfare he interposes.

… "It was necessary for Christ to become a real man, for as we are very far from God, we stand in a manner before Him in the person of our Priest, which could not be were He not one of us. Hence, that the Son of God has a nature in common with us does not diminish His dignity, but commends it the more to us; for He is fitted to reconcile us to God, because He is man" (John Calvin). [41]

If the Son of God had never become man, He could never have been a priest or performed any priestly functions. He could have taught us about his Father and instructed us in the just requirement of the Law, but he would never have been able to offer that sacrifice for the sins of His people which divine justice required. It was essential that "God became flesh and dwelt among us" if an eternal salvation was to be secured for God's elect.

The phrase, "is appointed to represent them" in verse one is important. It shows that the high priest was "appointed by God" for his office. He did not take a series of psychological tests to see if he had certain talents and a correct psychological make-up; he did not one day "feel led of the Lord" to make the high priestly work his calling. No, no, God personally chose, appointed, called and equipped the high priest for his

---

[41] Ibid., 139.

work. The reason why, and the purpose for which, the high priest was selected "from among men" is so that he might transact on behalf of others, or more accurately, in the stead of others.

The application of the words, "is appointed to represent them" to our new covenant high priest demonstrates the person and work of Christ. He not only became man, he received appointment from God to act on behalf of, in the stead of, men. He came to do the Father's will, "Here I am, I have come to do your will" (Heb. 10:9). This text not only announces the commission he received from God, it also asserts his readiness to discharge it. The will of God for Christ was the cross. He was born for the express purpose of dying. Our Lord was the only person who was ever born in order that he might die. We were born to live, but he was born to die. He came to do what needed to be done and no one but he could do it if there was to be a gospel to preach. He came to do what no man could do—satisfy the claims of divine justice, procure the divine favor.

Pink correctly notes in passing what the Holy Spirit specifically says, "'ordained for men,' not mankind in general, but that people whom God had given Him—just as Aaron, the typical high priest, confessed not the sins of the Canaanites or Amalekites over the head of the goat, but those of Israel only."[42]

"In things pertaining to God," that is, in meeting the requirements of His holiness. The activities of the priests have God for their object: it is His character, His claims, His glory which are in view. In their application to Christ these words, "in things pertaining to God" distinguishes our Lord's priesthood from His other offices. As a prophet, He reveals to *us* the mind and will of God. As the King, He subdues us to Himself,

---

[42] Ibid., 140.

rules over and *defends us*. But the object of His priesthood is not us, but God.[43]

We must always remember the difference between a prophet and a priest. A prophet represents God to men and a priest represents men to God.

The truth of Christ's humanity is not stressed as much as it should be. There is the tendency to get so involved in defending the truth of the deity of Christ that we neglect his humanity. It is just as vital that Christ be the son of Mary as it is that he be the Son of God. The following is a short excerpt from an excellent message which was on the internet on the humanity of Christ.

The ramifications of this truth [humanity of Christ] are many. For example: Christ's two natures can be distinguished but not separated.

Christ became something He never was before while never ceasing to be what he always was.

Christ has only one personality.

Christ's humanity never had an independent existence.

Christ is not able to sin, any more than God can sin.

Christ's humanity is not independent of His deity.

Christ never does anything 'as man' or 'as God' - He acts as Christ, who is God manifest in flesh.

After coming to earth at Bethlehem, Christ could no longer act solely 'as God.' Nor did He experience thirst and weariness solely 'as man.' He cannot act as man without being God - He cannot act as God without being man. The Lord said "I am thirsty" not "my human nature is thirsty." He said "I forgive"

---

43 Ibid., 140, 141.

not "my divine nature forgives you." It is vital never to divide the Lord Jesus in a way that Scripture does not allow. [44]

"... to offer gifts and sacrifice for sins" (Heb. 5:1b). This statement emphasizes an important fact that is not emphasized enough today. Christ offers himself to the Father before he is presented to sinners. This text shows that the sacrificial death of Christ was a priestly act. He offered something to God. He offered himself. He lay down his life in a conscious act of sacrifice for sins. This was not the work of a prophet or a king; it was the work of a priest. At Calvary the Lord Jesus was not only the sacrifice, the Lamb of God bearing judgment, but he was also the priest officiating at the altar. Our Lord offered his sinless life on the altar of his absolute deity and accomplished a perfect redemption for us poor sinners. Later, the writer will emphasize the necessity of Christ having an offering to give to God. "For every high priest is appointed to offer gifts and sacrifices; thus it is necessary for this priest also to have something to offer" (Heb. 8:3). Hebrews 9:14 tells us that our Lord "offered himself without blemish to God."

God gave his son up to the cross. It was the Father who put Christ on the cross. It was the Father's plan to have Christ die, and it was the Father's sovereign control that engineered the cross from beginning to end. No event was ever planned and executed as carefully as the death of Christ was planned and executed by the triune God. However, the Son of God readily agreed to "do the Father's will." Pink said it well:

> Christ on the Cross was far more than a willing victim passively enduring the stroke of Divine judgment. He was there *performing* a work, nor did He cease until He cried in triumph, "It is finished." He "loved the Church and *gave* Himself for it"

---

[44] Michael J. Penfield, "The Humanity of Christ"
(*http://www.webtruth.org/articles/christology-33/the-humanity-of-christ-70.html*) page no longer available, (7/30/2014).

(Eph. 5:25). He *"laid down* His life" for the sheep (John 10:11, 18)—which is the predicate of an active agent. He *"poured out* His soul unto death"* (Isa. 53:12).[45]

Hebrews 5:2 emphasizes that compassion is one of the sure results that will be evident in a true high priest. This same mark of compassion will be seen in anyone who has truly been called and ordained by God to function as a church leader. "He is able to deal gently with those who are ignorant and are going astray, since he himself is subject to weakness." The ignorant may be described as those who sin because they simply do not know any better. Their problem is ignorance of the truth. They may be new or untaught believers. Those who have "going astray" may be those who know better but deliberately choose to go their own way. Regardless of which it is the true minister of Christ feels compassion. He never excuses sin in any way, but he feels true sympathy. If the only feeling a leader feels when someone under his care goes astray is anger, that leader is a false shepherd.

1 Samuel 1:9-14 records the miserable failure of Eli the priest. When poor Hannah was "in bitterness of soul," and while she was in prayer, weeping before the Lord, "her lips were moving, but her voice was not heard," Eli thought that she was drunken, and spoke roughly to her. Thus, instead of sympathizing with her sorrows, instead of making intercession for her, he cruelly misjudged her. It is a strange anomaly, but it seems that the more doctrinally orthodox people become, the more they lose compassion. They become more interested in protecting the image of the institution than they do in helping poor sinners.

"This compassionate, loving, gentle, all-considerate and tender regard for the sinner can exist in perfection only in a sinless one. This appears at first sight paradoxical; for we expect the

---

[45] Pink, *Hebrews*, 141.

perfect man to be the severest judge. And with regard to *sin,* this is doubtless true. God charges even His angels with folly. He beholds sin where we do not discover it. And Jesus, the Holy One of Israel, like the Father, has eyes like a flame of fire, and discerns everything that is contrary to God's mind and will. But with regard to the *sinner,* Jesus, by virtue of His perfect holiness, is the most merciful, compassionate, and considerate Judge. For we, not taking a deep and keen view of sin, that central essential evil which exists in all men, and manifests itself in various ways and degrees, are not able to form a just estimate of men's comparative guilt and blameworthiness. Nay, our very sins make us more impatient and severe with regard to the sins of others. Our vanity finds the vanity of others intolerable, our pride finds the pride of others excessive. Blind to the guilt of our own peculiar sins, we are shocked with another's sins, different indeed from ours, but not less offensive to God, or pernicious in its tendencies. Again, the greater the knowledge of Divine love and pardon, the stronger faith in the Divine mercy and renewing grace, the more hopeful and the more lenient will be our view of sinners. And finally the more we possess of the spirit and heart of the Shepherd, the Physician, the Father, the deeper will be our compassion on the ignorant and wayward. [46]

One of the inconsistencies that amazes me is how clearly the Scriptures teach that Christ "loves the sinner but hates his sin." I am aware this truth has been greatly misused, and it usually winds up in a distorted "half-truth" form, but it is nonetheless a biblical fact that Jesus was perfectly clear in his hatred of sin and at the same time was tender and compassionate to the sinner. If you can't fit that into your theology, you need to revise your theology. Despite how holy he was Jesus still often revealed less shock toward the drunkard and profligate than the respectable, selfish, and ungodly religionists. I hate to say it, but I have met many Reformed elders who

---

[46] Ibid., 142.

exhibit most of the characteristics of the Pharisees in the New Testament. They view biblical compassion as a form of compromise. Jesus looked upon sin as the greatest and most fearful evil, and at the same time he saw the sinner as poor, lost, and helpless. He saw the just destruction of Jerusalem at the door, but still wept over its coming destruction. Hyper-Calvinism is always stingy with the love of God. It is far better at condemning than it is at reconciliation. It knows how to preach wrath but stumbles and gets tongue-tied with the love of God.

Hymn writer Frank Graeff got it pretty close.

Does Jesus care when my heart is pained
Too deeply for mirth or song;
As the burdens press, and the cares distress,
And the way grows weary and long?

Refrain:
Oh, yes, He cares, I know He cares!
His heart is touched with my grief;
When the days are weary, the long nights dreary,
I know my Savior cares.

Does Jesus care when my way is dark
With a nameless dread and fear?
As the daylight fades into deep night shades,
Does He care enough to be near?

Does Jesus care when I've tried and failed
To resist some temptation strong;
When for my deep grief there is no relief,
Though my tears flow all the night long?

Does Jesus care when I've said "goodbye"
To the dearest on earth to me,
And my sad heart aches till it nearly breaks—
Is it aught to Him? Does He see?

Christ,
A Priest Like Melchizedek
Chapter 10

Melchizedek is one of the most mysterious persons in all of Scripture. He seems to come from nowhere, makes one brief appearance, and then totally disappears without leaving a forwarding address. His whole history is recorded in three verses in the Old Testament Scriptures:

> Then Melchizedek king of Salem brought out bread and wine. He was priest of God Most High, and he blessed Abram, saying,
> "Blessed be Abram by God Most High,
> Creator of heaven and earth.
> And blessed be God Most High,
> who delivered your enemies into your hand."
>
> Then Abram gave him a tenth of everything (Gen. 14:18-21).

David makes the only other reference to Melchizedek in the Old Testament Scriptures. David, speaking prophetically, ties Melchizedek to the coming Messiah:

> The Lord has sworn
> and will not change his mind:
> "You are a priest forever,
> in the order of Melchizedek" (Ps. 110:4).

Nothing else is recorded about this mysterious person in the Old Testament Scriptures. The Jewish commentators take little note of Melchizedek in all of their writings. The writer of the book of Hebrews sees Melchizedek as one of the most important persons in the Old Testament Scriptures. Actually he is shown to be a greater person than even the patriarch Abraham. Melchizedek is also seen as the ultimate proof that our Lord is not only a true high priest, but he is a much greater high priest than was Aaron. Melchizedek thus becomes an extremely important man in the New Testament theology of fulfillment. There is a sense in which this mysterious man is the bridge between the two testaments. Melchizedek is the clear proof that the old covenant made with Israel at Sinai was an inferior and temporary arrangement that has been replaced by a new arrangement that is in reality older than the Mosaic covenant. The message taught in Hebrews concerning Melchizedek leaves the wavering Jews without any excuse for even thinking about going back to Judaism.

Hebrews introduces Melchizedek to the New Testament.

> *And he says in another place,*
>
> *"You are a priest forever,*
> *in the order of Melchizedek"* (Heb. 5:6).

The writer quickly notes an important bit of information about the attitude of the Jews toward Melchizedek. They did not like to hear about this mysterious person.

> *and, once made perfect, he became the source of eternal salvation for all who obey him and was designated by God to be high priest in the order of Melchizedek.*
>
> *We have much to say about this, but it is hard to explain because you are slow to learn* (Heb. 5:9-11).

The Jews' reluctance to hear about Melchizedek is at the heart of understanding the book of Hebrews. The exposition of the Melchizedek's role in redemptive history establishes the biblical relationship between the old and new covenants. The truth the Jews were not interested in hearing is the very foundation of our hope, as Gentiles, in Christ as the true Messiah. We will come back to this point in a moment and show that the book of Hebrews is a masterpiece of biblical exegesis. I used to say; "You could read those three verses about Melchizedek in Genesis 14 a million times and never come up with the theology of the book of Hebrews." Since learning new covenant theology I can see how wrong I was. Anyone using new covenant principles of exegesis will come to the same conclusions as this writer to the book of Hebrews. That is why the rabbinical writers are not interested in discussing Melchizedek. They can see where it leads and how clearly and thoroughly it ends the old covenant religion of Judaism it had established. We will come back to this after we demonstrate the importance of this mysterious person called Melchizedek.

Melchizedek Is a Type of Christ

First of all, we must realize that Melchizedek is a biblical "type" of Christ. A type is an Old Testament person or event that gives us a picture of a New Testament truth. A type usually foreshadows the person or work of Christ. The bronze serpent that Moses had placed on a pole was a type of Christ being lifted up on the cross to bear our guilt. This is not just our idea, but it is specifically set forth in the New Testament Scriptures:

> *Just as Moses lifted up the snake in the desert, so the Son of Man must be lifted up,* (John 3:14).

As we read the Old Testament Scriptures we will often see things that clearly remind us of something about Christ, and we call this a "type of Christ." However, a biblical type of Christ will always have a reference in the New Testament Scriptures that informs us what the type in the Old Testament Scriptures means. John 3:14 proves that Numbers 21:8 is to be understood as a type of Christ's atoning work. Jonah being in the whale's belly is specifically mentioned in the New Testament Scriptures as a type of Christ's burial and resurrection. The lambs slain by the old covenant priests were types of Christ, the true Lamb of God. John 1:29 states this clearly. Hebrews 7:1-3 tells us that the Melchizedek mentioned in Genesis and Psalms is a type of Christ as our High Priest.

Types are very limited in their use in that they give us only a very small aspect of the thing which they typify. For instance both Aaron and Melchizedek are types of different aspects of Christ's high priestly work, but in Hebrews 7:1-10 the writer's whole point is to show how totally inferior Aaron is to Melchizedek even though Aaron is a true type of Christ. Sometimes a type of Christ will only show one particular thing about him or his saving work.

The first thing to understand is that Hebrews 7:3 is clearly stating that Melchizedek is a type of Christ.

Melchizedek's Identity - Who, or What, is He?

Some commentators believe Melchizedek was an angel, others that this was a pre-incarnate appearance of Christ on earth, and still others insist that Melchizedek was a real historical man. The evidence of the latter seems to me to be conclusive.

First of all, Melchizedek is said to be "like the Son of God" (Heb. 7:3). The writer would not say that if Melchizedek was in reality the Son of God but merely "like" him. Secondly, one of the specific requirements for anyone being a high priest was that the individual had to be a true human being.

Every high priest is selected from among men and is appointed to represent them in matters related to God, to offer gifts and sacrifices for sins (Heb. 5:1).

The whole argument of Hebrews 4:14-16 is designed to prove that the humanity of Christ is the foundational truth that gives us the courage to come to him with absolute assurance that he understands us and can help us. It can be argued that if Melchizedek is not a real human being, then he lacks the essential qualifications of being a high priest. If Melchizedek is in reality Christ himself, then there is no legitimate human priesthood "after the order of Melchizedek." However, the most important reason for believing Melchizedek is a real human being is the point the writer is proving by associating Melchizedek with Christ as a High Priest. Remember that the writer of Hebrews is showing that the new covenant believer not only has a real High Priest, but our high priest is of an order that predates the Levitical priesthood. In fact, both Aaron and Abraham, the patriarch himself, paid tithes to a priest in the same order as our High Priest. More later!

I am sure many will ask, "But how do you understand the language used in Hebrews 7:3? Those things can only apply to Christ." Let us look at the text carefully.

> *Without father or mother, without genealogy, without beginning of days or end of life, like the Son of God he remains a priest forever* (Heb. 7:3).

The writer is not comparing two men but two kinds of priesthood. This fact unlocks the meaning of the passage. All of the things said about Melchizedek are exactly opposite of the Levitical priests. When we compare Melchizedek as a priest to a Levitical priest, then Christ is totally different than the Levitical priesthood, and he is like the Melchizedek priesthood. If this verse is comparing Melchizedek the man to Jesus the man then the words cannot possibly describe our Lord. Jesus, the man, had a mother, and his "beginning of days" or birth is one of the most clearly established facts in history—we celebrate it at Christmas time. His "end of days" is a public event that actually took place in history. Besides all of that, the two genealogies of Christ are carefully traced in the New Testament Scriptures. The man, Jesus, has a clear and recorded genealogy. Let's look at the things in the text one at time.

First of all, ancestry was a big deal at that point in history. It meant everything in the Levitical order of priests. An event in the time of Ezra proves this point.

> *And from among the priests:*

The descendants of

Hobaiah, Hakkoz and Barzillai (a man who had married a daughter of Barzillai the Gileadite and was called by that name).

These searched for their family records, but they could not find them and so were excluded from the priesthood as unclean. The governor ordered them not to eat any of the most sacred food until there was a priest ministering with the Urim and Thummim (Ezra 2:61-63).

These priests were considered "polluted" and were not allowed to function until a testimony from God verified their heredity.

Secondly, the whole tribe of Levi was assigned to do the work of the Tabernacle. They alone were allowed into the Holy Place. Everyone else was shut out, or they would be put to death.

Give the Levites to Aaron and his sons; they are the Israelites who are to be given wholly to him. Appoint Aaron and his sons to serve as priests; anyone else who approaches the sanctuary must be put to death." (Num. 3:9-10).

Jesus himself could not have ministered in the priestly temple service since he was not a Levite. Remember that God killed Nadab and Abihu, the two sons of Aaron, for daring to perform unauthorized ceremonies in the Holy Place.

Thirdly, all priests were Levites but not all Levites were priests. Most of the Levites "waited on the sons of Aaron." Only the sons of Aaron were priests, and the rest of the Levites took care of the Tabernacle, the grounds, and any other work associated with the Tabernacle. The priests began their priestly functions at age thirty, and they retired at age fifty.

Count all the men from thirty to fifty years of age who come to serve in the work in the Tent of Meeting.

"This is the work of the Kohathites in the Tent of Meeting: the care of the most holy thing" (Num. 4:3-5).

Aaron's sons did not begin their life at age thirty, but they did begin their priestly work at age thirty, and they ended that work at age fifty.

The significance of the words in the beginning of Hebrews 7:3 is not that "Melchizedek, like Jesus, had no father, no mother, and no human descent." That could not be true as we have just demonstrated. The writer is saying, "Melchizedek is a priest of an order where natural descent has nothing at all to do with his being a priest. Melchizedek is a priest by virtue of his own person and by God's sovereign calling." The Levitical restrictions have no more to do with Melchizedek than they have to do with Christ.

The later part of the verse is not saying that Melchizedek was never born, or that he never died (Jesus was born and he died); rather, Melchizedek's priesthood had no time or age restrictions. He "remains a priest (not a man) forever" (not eternally) which means his priesthood did not, like the elliptical priesthood, end when he was fifty years old. Melchizedek became a priest by God's sovereign appointment with no reference at all to genealogy, and he continued in a perpetual priesthood as long as he lived. So does our High Priest, and since he truly does live forever to make intercession for us, we too will live forever.

It is significant that Melchizedek was both a king and a priest. Under the Law of Moses this was not allowed. But Christ, like Melchizedek, is both King and Priest. Zechariah 6:12-13 clearly foretold that the Messiah would be both King and Priest.

It is also clear from the titles given to Melchizedek that he is a type of Christ. He is King of Righteousness and King of Peace. It is only at the cross that these two things meet (see Psalm 85:10). John 3:16 is text that declares both God's holy love and his holy wrath. His holy love gave his Son up to the death on the cross. God's giving his Son up to death on the cross made his love possible. The cross satisfied God's righteousness. Understanding the fact that God is satisfied with Christ's atonement is what gives us assurance that we are acceptable in God's sight. We are just as acceptable to God as is his son. Notice the correct order. Righteousness is the only foundation for true peace. We can only be satisfied when we are acceptable with God as we see ourselves united to Christ in his death, burial and resurrection.

In one sense, it is surprising that Jewish writers say so little about Melchizedek. You would think they would love to be intrigued with the obvious obscurity of these few verses. The writer of the book of Hebrews builds the whole authority for Christ's ministry as High Priest on the three verses from Genesis and the one verse in the Psalms.

Why is Melchizedek so Important?

Hebrews 7:4 raises and answers that very question. The main purpose of this section in Hebrews is not to show that Melchizedek is greater than Aaron. It does that very clearly, but it does it in a way designed to show that Melchizedek is also greater than Abraham himself. The main purpose of the writer of Hebrews in this section is to show that the gospel of grace not only predates both Moses and Aaron, but it also predates the patriarch Abraham himself. The religion that we espouse was in existence long before Israel and Judaism existed. The gospel of sovereign grace is not integrally connected to anything that is Jewish. This is a masterful argument. What is essential to see is that everything in the old covenant, including the basic covenant document itself, is finished, and in each case something much better has taken its place.

1:1–Christ is superior to all of the Old Testament prophets - 1:1-3

1:4–Christ is superior to the Angels–1:4-2:18

3:3–Christ is superior to Moses–3:1-6

4:8, 9–Christ is superior to the Sabbath–4:1-11

4:8, 9–Christ is superior to Joshua–4:1-11

8:6–Christ is superior to Aaron–4:14-10:25

The Jew might be ready to respond, "Yes, but what about our father Abraham? Where is it claimed that Christ was greater than Abraham?" This writer responds to this possible objection. "Have you not read how Abraham was blessed by a priest after the order of our High Priest? Surely you agree that the lesser is always blessed by the greater. You also know that Aaron, your High Priest, actually paid tithes, because he was in Abraham's loins at the time, to a priest named Melchizedek." The crowning argument of this section is that Melchizedek's blessing of Abraham and receiving tithes from him is positive proof that Melchizedek is greater than Abraham himself, and Christ is greater than Melchizedek. We must see this master stroke in the argument of the book of Hebrews.

Before we come down too hard on these people who are "slow to learn," must we not admit we are the same way? It is a very short step to move from traditions to traditionalism. Some people do not "feel" they have "really worshipped" if either the music or worship format was "different from their Church." It is amazing how "slow to learn (dull of hearing, ESV)" we become when we hear something that isn't part of our particular creed or that our favorite preacher has never mentioned. It was a failure to keep looking to Jesus alone that created the problem of slowness in these Hebrews.

The Setting and Context

Before we look at these verses about Melchizedek in detail, let me remind you of the setting and purpose of the letter to the Hebrews. Many Jews believed that Jesus was the Messiah and that he had died and risen again from the dead. They believed he had ascended into heaven. They had accepted these facts as true. The problem with many of these "believers" was their refusal to accept the clear implications and certain consequences that flowed from those facts. If Calvary was the true and final Day of Atonement, and if Christ had indeed risen from the dead and ascended into the true Most Holy Place, and if the rending of the veil was the voice of God from heaven ending the old covenant and all of its attendants, then it follows that Christ is our true Great High Priest in God's presence, and Aaron and Judaism are finished. Aaron has been replaced, and Judaism and all it stood for is gone.

If all of this is true, then Aaron, the Prophets, the temple worship, the sacrifices, the holy days and holy places have all been done away and been replaced with the reality that they were only a "shadow" or type. A.W. Pink has said it well:

> At Hebrews 5:11 the apostle declared, "Of whom we have many things to say and hard to be uttered, seeing ye are dull of hearing". The difficulty lay in the strong disinclination of man to relinquish that which has long been cherished, which nowhere appears more evident than in connection with religious things. To say that Christ was a High Priest "after the order of *Melchizedek*" was tantamount to affirming that the *Aaronic* order was Divinely set aside, and with it, all the ordinances and ceremonies of the Mosaic law. "This," …, "was the hardest thing of all for a Hebrew, even a converted one, to bow to, for it meant repudiating everything that was seen, and cleaving to that which was altogether invisible. It meant forsaking that which their fathers had honored for fifteen hundred years, and espousing that which the great majority of their brethren according to the flesh denounced as Satanic."[47]

It is interesting that Pink, an ardent covenant theologian, cannot bring himself to say, "The Mosaic Law (or even "the old covenant") is set aside. It was not only the "ordinances and ceremonies" that were done away at the cross, but the

---

[47] Ibid., 357.

whole Law covenant, including the Tables of the Covenant, or Ten Commandments, were all done away and replaced with a "better covenant" (Heb. 8:6). Christ canceled the written code (Tablets of Stone), with its regulations, (whole Law of Moses) that was against us and that stood opposed to us. He took it (the "written code that was against us") away, nailing it to the cross" (Col. 2:14). The text clearly distinguishes between the "written code" (Tables of the Covenant) and the "regulations" that administered that covenant. See the same truth set forth in Hebrews 9:1-4.

The Greatness of Our High Priest

In Hebrews 2:17 the writer introduces Christ's priesthood. He emphasizes the merciful and sympathetic character of our Priest. It is this that gives us confidence to draw near and find grace to help in time of need. In Hebrews 5:1 we are reminded that a priest was neither a prophet nor a king. His primary function was to represent men to God. The prophet represented God to man and said, "Thus saith the Lord." The priest offered "gifts and sacrifices" to God and made intercession for those for whom the offering was made. The two things essential in the priest's ministry were to make atonement and then to intercede. In Hebrews 2:17 the writer emphasizes that the priest's ministry was "in service to God" by "making atonement for sins."

Now it follows that if the whole purpose and function of the priesthood was to make an atonement for sins, and further, if that priesthood with all of its offering could not effect true atonement (all it could do was "cover over sin," and that for only a year) then it had to be replaced with a priesthood that could offer an acceptable sacrifice and accomplish the necessary work of true and eternal atonement.

Log this into your memory bank: The old priesthood, and everything associated with it, had to be discarded and totally replaced. It was not just altered, or updated, or even revised just a bit. It had to be totally done away with and replaced by something "better." It had to be done away because it was ineffective in bringing sinners into the most holy presence of God. The Aaronic priesthood could not offer a sacrifice that could pay the debt our sin incurred. Hebrews 2:17 is telling us that Christ is the first High Priest that could successfully make a true atonement for sinners. He is the first High Priest who could open the veil and give us assurance to "come boldly" into the presence of God.

Christ, Our Assurance
Chapter 11

Nothing demonstrates the superiority of the new covenant over the old covenant as much as the work of Christ as Priest when compared with the work of Aaron as Priest. Simply stated, Christ's work as our priest on the cross accomplished what Aaron was never able to accomplish. Christ offered a sacrifice, himself, that fully paid for sin and satisfied the holy character of God. Aaron could not offer such a sacrifice. He could not effect a true atonement for sin. Christ brings his people into the true Most Holy Place in heaven not only forgiven but also fully justified and robed in a perfect righteousness. Aaron could not himself enter the Most Holy Place let alone bring sinners into God's presence. A comparison of the doctrine of assurance under the old covenant with assurance under the new covenant will help us see this truth. David's confession of his adultery with Bathsheba and the murder of Uriah her husband, as recorded in Psalm 51, are most helpful in understanding the difference between the old and new doctrine of assurance of salvation.

I once heard a preacher say, "David's awful sin of adultery and murder proves the doctrine of eternal security." He was very wrong. David's sin does not prove eternal security, but Psalm 51 proves the grace of God toward David. All David's sin of adultery and murder proves is that he was a sinner like the rest of us. His recorded repentance in Psalm 51 proves he was a godly man despite the fact that he had succumbed to temptation and fallen into sin. His repentance described so vividly in Psalm 51 proves he was indeed a godly man in spite of his being overtaken in sin in a given instance. I am interested in showing how David's sin and repentance differs from sin and repentance under the new covenant.

David's sin of murder and adultery are recorded in II Samuel 11 and 12. We need not go over the sordid details of David's sin except to note that God makes no attempt to in any way spin the sins and failures of his saints, even the worst among them. We do everything possible to cover up and hide the sins of our heroes. God tells it like it is. Our Lord is not ashamed to call the worst of repentant sinners his brothers (Heb. 2:11). He does not make any attempt to rewrite the story of their lives. He admits his family is made up of the worst of sinners. In Psalm 51:1-3, David openly acknowledges his awful sin and his repentance. He makes no attempt to justify what he did. He pleads no extenuating circumstances but freely admits his awful sin.

Have mercy on me, O God,
according to your unfailing love;
according to your great compassion
blot out my transgressions.
Wash away all my iniquity
and cleanse me from my sin.
For I know my transgressions,
and my sin is always before me (Ps. 51:1-3).

In verse 4, David is not denying that he has sinned against both Bathsheba and Uriah. He sees his greatest sin is against God and his truth. The later part of verse 4 shows how clearly David understood the need for open confession. He wants to make sure that everyone realizes that whatever God chooses to do with him, he deserves it. This includes his being cast off by God if God so chose that punishment. David is concerned with vindicating God in any action God chose to take.

Against you, you only, have I sinned
and done what is evil in your sight,

so that you are proved right when you speak
and justified when you judge (Ps. 51:4).

Verses 5 to10 describe a man who feels the awful reality of his sin and depravity. He longs to be free from the power of indwelling sin. He is not satisfied in only being forgiven for two particular sins; he wants to be changed from the inside out. He frankly acknowledges both his sin and the depth of his total depravity. David is acknowledging that he was a sinner from his very conception. He was totally depraved from day one of his life.

Surely I was sinful at birth,
sinful from the time my mother conceived me.

Surely you desire truth in the inner parts; you teach me wisdom in
the inmost place.

Cleanse me with hyssop, and I will be clean;
wash me, and I will be whiter than snow.

Let me hear joy and gladness;
let the bones you have crushed rejoice.

Hide your face from my sins
and blot out all my iniquity.

Create in me a pure heart, O God,
and renew a steadfast spirit within me. (Ps. 51:5-10)

Verse 11 is a much-disputed verse. Those who confuse "eternal security" with the "perseverance of the saints" have real difficulty understanding this verse.

Do not cast me from your presence
or take your Holy Spirit from me (Ps. 51:11).

This text seems to be saying that a believer can lose his salvation. The text surely shows that David lost the assurance of his salvation. Let me make a few preliminary statements. David, in spite of his sin of adultery and murder, was just as eternally secure in his salvation as a believer is today. However, he had no way of knowing that fact. David believed he could lose his salvation even though he could not. When he prayed, "take not thy Holy Spirit from me, he really believed that it was possible for him to be "cast off" by God. David saw what happened to Saul and was deeply concerned that the same thing might happen to him. Saul was cast off and the Spirit was taken from him.

It is argued that in verse 12 he is praying to have the "joy of salvation" restored and not praying to have salvation itself restored. David's prayer in verse 11 proves he did not feel he had been cast off from God or that the Spirit had been taken from him. He is praying those things will not happen. He prayed as he did because he believed that both of those things could happen, and he believed that he deserved to have them both happen. Any consistent and fair exegesis of David's words proves that he clearly believed that he could be cast off by God and the Spirit be taken away from him. Because he believed these things had not yet happened, that does not mean that he understood they could never happen. David believed both of these things could happen, and he would be lost. David was praying that he would not lose his salvation. David did not believe he was eternally secure in his salvation even though he really was just as secure as a believer under the new covenant.

Verses 12 to 15 is a prayer for persevering grace and the resulting fruit of true repentance.

Restore to me the joy of your salvation and grant me a willing spirit, to sustain me.

Then I will teach transgressors your ways, and sinners will turn back to you.

Save me from bloodguilt, O God, the God who saves me, and my tongue will sing of your righteousness.

O Lord, open my lips, and my mouth will declare your praise (Ps. 51:12-15).

Verse 16 is one of the key verses in Psalm 51. This text throws a lot of light on new covenant theology.

> *You do not delight in sacrifice, or I would bring it;*
> *you do not take pleasure in burnt offerings.*

At first reading this verse presents a problem that only new covenant theology can resolve. David lived under the old covenant when sacrifices and burnt offerings were not only performed; they were commanded to be performed. God indeed desired sacrifice and burnt offerings under the old covenant. In some cases the failure to bring a prescribed sacrifice was punished with death. Why would David say that God did not desire sacrifices when he had clearly commanded them? The answer is simple. There was no sacrifice that David could bring for his particular sins! There was no sacrifice for murder or adultery under the old covenant. There was no sacrifice in the whole Mosaic system that covered adultery and murder. Hebrews 10:28 is quite clear. To willfully disobey the Law of Moses meant death with no questions asked. "Anyone who rejected the law of Moses died without mercy on the testimony of two or three witnesses" (Heb. 10:28).

There was nothing in the entire Mosaic Law, the whole old covenant that gave David the least assurance of forgiveness for his sins of adultery and murder. The sacrifice on the Day of Atonement did not apply to his condition. The sacrifice on the Day of Atonement was for the "sins committed in ignorance." That sacrifice did not cover sins that "rejected the Law," "Anyone who rejected the law of Moses died without mercy on the testimony of two or three witnesses" (Heb. 10:28). Hebrews 9 describes Aaron's work on the Day of Atonement. It clearly states that the atonement only covered sins "committed in ignorance." "But only the high priest entered the inner room, and that only once a year, and never without blood, which he offered for himself and for the sins the people had committed in ignorance" (Heb. 9:7).

Aaron could not help David. There was nothing in Aaron's bag of promises that offered forgiveness to a murderer and adulterer. Aaron's message to David was the message of Hebrews 10:28. Likewise the City of Refuge could not help him in the case of murder. A man who killed his neighbor accidently could flee to a city of refuge and escape the anger and revenge of the dead man's friends and relatives (see Num. 35:25 ff). However, if the death was deliberate and not accidental, the murderer was taken from the City of Refuge and turned over to the avenger of blood to be punished for committing murder (Deut. 19:11-13).

David totally by-passed the whole Mosaic system of sacrifices because nothing in that system could help him. He ignored Aaron and his entire priestly ministry because nothing in the old covenant under which Aaron ministered could give him any hope. David ignored Aaron and the whole old covenant and cried out to the God he knew as a shepherd boy and pleaded for his grace and mercy. God heard David and forgave him because God honors true repentance that bases its appeal on grace alone. When the Holy Spirit works a true "broken spirit" and "contrite heart" in a poor sinner's heart with no hope except sovereign grace, that sinner will never be cast off no matter what his sin.

The sacrifices of God are a broken spirit; a broken and contrite heart, O God, you will not despise.

In your good pleasure make Zion prosper; build up the walls of Jerusalem.

Then there will be righteous sacrifices, whole burnt offerings to delight you; then bulls will be offered on your altar (Ps 51:17-19).

When you compare a text like Psalm 51 with a New Testament text like 1 John 1:7-10, you see the difference in assurance under the new covenant as compared to assurance under the old covenant.

But if we walk in the light, as he is in the light, we have fellowship with one another, and the blood of Jesus, his Son, purifies us from all sin.

If we claim to be without sin, we deceive ourselves and the truth is not in us. If we confess our sins, he is faithful and just and will forgive us our sins and purify us from all unrighteousness. If we claim we have not sinned, we make him out to be a liar and his word has no place in our lives.

"Walking in the light" (v. 7a), is consciously obeying God. It is not sinless perfection but it is living in obedience where we are not conscious of specific sins. When we so live, we will have fellowship with God. The fact that we are not conscious of specific sins does not mean we are in any sense living a sinless life, it merely means that God has not convicted us of any specific sins. To think or say we have no sins would be to deceive ourselves (v. 8). If we confess the specific sins of which we are convicted, we are assured that God will forgive us (v. 9). We will still have sins that God has not yet convicted us of and they will also, like the "sins committed in ignorance" on the Day of Atonement, be forgiven. We will be cleansed of all unrighteousness and walk in fellowship with God. As we grow in grace the Holy Spirit will point out more and more sins of ignorance to us, and they will have to be confessed if we are to maintain our fellowship with God. This is not the same as maintaining our salvation.

The most important difference between Psalm 51 and 1 John 1:7-10 is the words in 1 John 1:7, "the blood of Jesus, his Son, purifies us from all sin." A new covenant believer's assurance of forgiveness is based on the fact that he knows all of his sin, past, present, and future is fully paid for by the atonement of Christ. A new covenant believer can never "come into condemnation" (John 5:24 and Romans 8:1). A new covenant believer can never come before God as a judge; he has not only already been judged and found to be guilty, he has already been put to death. He has died with Christ, been buried with Christ and been raised from the dead with Christ. He already is seated in heaven in Christ. He can never again be judged. All of his dealings with God are now that of a son born into the family of God. God is his Father, not a judge. The redeemed new covenant believer is a justified child of God and not a criminal. A believer today could not pray Psalm 51:11: "Do not cast me from your presence or take your Holy Spirit from me."

If I am united to Christ in his death, burial, resurrection and ascension, then I am already seated together with Christ in heaven. I can no more be cast off from God than Christ could be cast off.

David could not see himself as seated in heaven with Christ before Christ was literally ascended to heaven himself. Our knowledgeable experience cannot exceed the revelation which we have been given. We cannot read the experience of Romans 5:1; 8:1; John 5:24 and Ephesians 2:5-6 back into David's life and experience. Having a hope of a future blessing and experiencing the actual fulfillment of that blessing are two different things. A murderer on death row today may trust Christ and be saved. In spite of his sin of murder, he is included in the promises just listed. He will be saved if he claims, by a faith wrought in him by the Holy Spirit, the promise of salvation. He will be able to claim I John 1:9 in the same way and to the same degree as any other believer. David, as a murderer and adulterer living under the old covenant, did not have such a promise. He could not claim the promises of Romans 5:1; 8:1; John 5:24 and Ephesians 2:5-6. Those are new covenant promises and could not have been made until Christ established the new covenant in his blood. David's hope was not in a specific promise since he had no such promise as a murderer and adulterer under the old covenant. David's hope lay in the character of the God he had communed with as a youth while tending his father's sheep.

There is a major difference in the concept of God and his relationship to his people in the old covenant and the new covenant. This difference is highlighted by J.I. Packer in his superb book *Knowing God*. If I could get every Christian to read only three books, *Knowing God* would one of them. It is worth its weight in gold!

Packer correctly sees the deep distinction between the revelation in the New Testament of God as a heavenly Father and the Old Testament revelation of God as a covenant God.

> You sum up the whole of New Testament teaching in a single phrase, if you speak of it as a revelation of the Fatherhood of the holy Creator. In the same way, you sum up the whole of New Testament religion if you describe it as the knowledge of God as one's Holy Father. If you want to judge how well a person understands Christianity, find out how much he makes of the thought of being God's child, and having God as his Father. If this is not the thought that prompts and controls his worship and prayers and his whole outlook on life, it means that he does not understand Christianity very well at all. For everything that Christ taught, everything that makes the New Testament new, and better than the Old, everything that is distinctively Christian as opposed to merely Jewish, is summed up in the knowledge of the Fatherhood of God. 'Father' is the Christian name for God. [48]

David did not grasp the full truth of the Fatherhood of God, but he surely had a glimpse of it. In his heart he was far ahead of the old covenant. His fellowship with God as he had revealed himself in creation enabled him to hope in God's

---

[48] J.I. Packer, *Knowing God* (Downers Grove, IL: InterVarsity Press, 1993), 201.

grace and mercy without a specific promise. David's relationship with God was not at all typical of an Old Covenant believer. He never used the word *Father* but he surely talked to God as a Father.

Christ,
Our New Covenant Lord
Chapter 12

Thus far we have looked at Christ our New Covenant Prophet and our New Covenant Priest. With this chapter we begin to look at Christ, our New Covenant King. The kingship of Christ is the most controversial of all the three offices because it directly involves ones prophetic view. We need to define what we mean when we refer to Christ as "our King." There are quite a few references to "Christ, the King of the Jews" in the New Testament, but there are only three direct references to Christ as "King" in the New Testament, and all three of those combine the word "King" and the word "Lord". Christ is said to be "Lord of Lord and King of Kings." Some dispensationalists insist that Christ is not presently King. They will speak of "Christ Our Prophet, Priest and coming King." This grows out of their dispensational belief that Christ at his first coming offered the promised kingdom to the Jews, and they rejected it. The kingdom was "postponed" and will be established at the second coming of Christ. They insist that Christ is Lord over the Church and King over a future converted nation of Israel. I believe the promised kingdom has already come, and Jesus is presently seated on the throne of David as King. We will use the terms "King" and "Lord" as synonyms in this article.

On his robe and on his thigh he has this name written:
KING OF KINGS AND LORD OF LORDS. (Rev. 19:16).

They will make war against the Lamb, but the Lamb will overcome them because he is Lord of lords and King of kings—and with him will be his called, chosen and faithful followers (Rev. 17:14).

which he will display at the proper time—he who is the blessed and only Sovereign, the King of kings and Lord of lords, (1 Tim. 6:15 ESV).

We should note that some secular kings have called themselves "King of Kings and Lord of Lords." The title is meant to show that the one bearing it is the highest authority. He is Lord over everyone and all things. Only one person has the right to wear that title, and that is the one who was God manifest in human flesh. Jesus, our New Covenant King died, rose from the dead, ascended into heaven and is presently seated on a throne at the right hand of God the Father. Our Lord is not only the King of the Jews, but he is also the King of the universe and everything in it. Acts Chapter 2 is a very key section of Scripture dealing with our subject. Let me repeat a small part of it.

> *"Brothers, I can tell you confidently that the patriarch David died and was buried, and his tomb is here to this day. But he was a prophet and knew that God had promised him on oath that he would place one of his descendants on his throne. Seeing what was ahead, he spoke of the resurrection of the Christ, that he was not abandoned to the grave, nor did his body see decay. God has raised this Jesus to life, and we are all witnesses of the fact. Exalted to the right hand of God, he has received from the Father the promised Holy Spirit and has poured out what you now see and hear. For David did not ascend to heaven, and yet he said,*
> *"'The Lord said to my Lord:*
> *"Sit at my right hand*
> *until I make your enemies*
> *a footstool for your feet."'*
> *"Therefore let all Israel be assured of this: God has made this Jesus, whom you crucified, both Lord and Christ"* (Acts 2:29-36).

The key verse is this quotation is verse 36. His Father in heaven raised the "same Jesus," the son of Mary, which the Jews crucified from the dead. The Father rewarded his Son for his redemptive work by exalting him to the highest place of authority. He made him, that same Jesus, son of Mary, to be the Lord of the universe and the Savior of God's elect. One of my favorite choruses is "He is Lord."

He is Lord, He is Lord, He has risen from the dead and He is Lord.

Every knee shall bow, Every tongue confess that Jesus Christ is Lord.

We should note that preaching the Gospel involves preaching that Jesus Christ is Lord and calling sinners to bow to Christ as Lord in repentance and faith. The important thing is to see that the Lordship we are talking about is an earned Lordship. Christ was always the Son of God or second person of the trinity just as he was always Lord of all creation; however, the Father rewarded his redemptive work as the Messiah with the new authority described in John.

> *After Jesus said this, he looked toward heaven and prayed:*
>
> *"Father, the time has come. Glorify your Son, that your Son may glorify you. For you granted him authority over all people that he might give eternal life to all those you have given him. Now this is eternal life: that they may know you, the only true God, and Jesus Christ, whom you have sent. I have brought you glory on earth by completing the work you gave me to do* (John 17:1-4).

Our Lord, in his humanity, was a man under specific orders. He came into the world with a specific job description (John 17:4) that culminated in the cross. Christ was born for the express idea of dying under the wrath of God as a sin offering. It was the Father who put him on the cross, and it was also the Father who raised him from the dead and "gave him all authority"(John 17:2). Several things must be noted.

1.   "The work" our Lord was commissioned to perform was the work of redemption. It was to provide for the elect all they needed to stand fully justified in God's holy presence. It involved the "doing and dying of Christ." It included keeping the Law and earning the righteousness it promised and then

dying under the curse of the Law and fully paying our debt of sin.

2.   That redemptive work was finished when Jesus cried out on the cross, "It is finished."

3.   The Father was satisfied with that redemptive work and rewarded Christ for performing that work by raising him from the dead, seating him on a throne at his own right hand and giving him authority over all flesh. The "all flesh" included all men without exception.

4.   The authority that was given to Christ was the legal authority to justly forgive sinners. He could only forgive sinners because he had offered to God his Father an acceptable sacrifice for sins and a perfect sinless life of obedience.

5.   We keep insisting that Christ's Lordship, or authority, which we are discussing is an earned authority. We are not saying or in any way suggesting that this reward in any way adds to Christ's deity. We are not talking about Christ's deity as opposed to his humanity. Christ's atoning work on the cross added nothing to the deity of Christ. That redemptive work did give Christ, acting in his humanity as our substitute, the legal right to forgive sins. That work satisfied the holy character of God. No one, including God, can arbitrarily forgive sins without a righteous basis. Paul, in Romans 1:16-17 and 3:24-26, makes it abundantly clear that the Gospel "justifies God in his justifying sinners." The Gospel shows that sin must be paid for before a holy God can forgive them. The death, resurrection and ascension of Christ provide the essential work of redemption that make it possible for God to be both "just and the justifier" of those for whom Christ died. Paul insists that the gospel reveals the righteousness of God (Rom. 1:17). Christ's "work" on the cross is where "righteousness and peace kiss each other" (Psalm 85:10).

6.   Christ earned the Lordship, or authority, to forgive sinners in his humanity. Christ's redemption involved both his deity and his humanity. Evangelicals have a tendency to forget that both Christ's holy life that earned righteousness and his obedient death that paid for sin were both performed in a human sinless body. Our Redeemer and Savior is not only the Son of God, but he is also the son of Mary. Our substitute is both deity and human. The work of our salvation involves both the Son of God and the son of Mary. It involves both of these, and both are vital.

We believe and preach both the humanity and deity of Christ. If we lose either the deity of Christ or his sinless humanity, we will have a heretical view of Christ's person and work. Hebrews 4:14-16 would lose its power to help us in time of need if Christ is not one with us in his humanity. Romans 8:28 would be a mere sentimental platitude if Christ is not both a sovereign deity and our human brother. Sometimes both Christ's deity and his humanity are emphasized in the same passage.

> A furious squall came up, and the waves broke over the boat, so that it was nearly swamped. Jesus was in the stern, sleeping on a cushion. The disciples woke him and said to him, "Teacher, don't you care if we drown?"

> He got up, rebuked the wind and said to the waves, "Quiet! Be still!" Then the wind died down and it was completely calm.

> He said to his disciples, "Why are you so afraid? Do you still have no faith?"

> They were terrified and asked each other, "Who is this? Even the wind and the waves obey him!" (Mark 4:37-41).

Why was Jesus sleeping? The answer simple, he was sleeping for the same reason we go to sleep. He was tired and his body needed rest. He was a man, a human being. But wait a minute. How could a mere man calm the raging sea with nothing but a verbal command? Because he was more than a mere man; he was the Son of God. He was deity made flesh. He was the God-man.

We are not talking about "deity versus humanity." We are talking about an earned Lordship that was given to Christ Jesus the God-man as a reward for finishing the work his Father gave him to do.

Nearly all Christians agree that the three offices of Prophet, Priest, and King set forth in the Old Testament Scriptures are types of the work and ministry of the Messiah which are fulfilled in the past and present ministry of our Lord Jesus Christ. 1 Corinthians 1:30 is one of many texts.

> *It is because of him that you are in Christ Jesus, who has become for us wisdom from God—that is, our righteousness, holiness and redemption.*

Wisdom refers to his work as Prophet to teach us about God and ourselves. Righteousness is his work of Priest to remove our guilt and justify us in God's sight. Sanctification is his work through his office as King, or Lord, to rule over us and conquer sin in us. Redemption is the full and final work of a complete salvation that involves all three offices of Christ's work. That work accomplishes a deliverance from the penalty, power, and finally even the presence of sin. This whole work of a complete and eternal salvation is "of him" and not of us.

In our booklet, *Christ, Lord and Lawgiver over the Church*[49] we discussed four things about the Lordship of Christ: (1) Its NATURE; (2) Its EXTENT; (3) How It Is EXERCISED or Mediated; (4) Modern Examples of Denying Christ's Lordship. It is most helpful in understanding the subject under discussion. The Lordship of Christ that we are discussing in this

---

[49] John G. Reisinger, *Christ, Lord and Lawgiver over the Church* (Frederick, MD: New Covenant Media, 1998), 1, 2, 3, 6.

chapter is an earned Lordship and is part of the nature of the Lordship of Christ. I emphasize again that this is not part of his deity as such. This is the authority and power given to "the man Christ Jesus" by the Father to save or damn whom he will. John's words cannot be understood any other way. Notice two texts:

> For you granted him authority over all people that he might give eternal life to all those you have given him (John 17:2).

Jesus alone has the authority (legal right) to justly and righteously forgive sins because he has paid for those sins. Jesus Christ is the only man who can forgive sins, and he is also the only man who can send anyone to hell! And he must do either one or the other with every person. All people, without exception, are in the hands of Jesus Christ the judge. See Acts 17:31.

I am often amazed at how preachers can so grossly misuse a text of Scripture. This is especially true when they butcher texts that deal with the sovereignty of God. The short dialogue between Pilate and Jesus is a classic example. This is one the favorite passages for Arminian evangelists. They use it as part of an altar call. They say, "Jesus is in your hands to do with as you choose. What will you do with Jesus?" I have yet to hear a single Arminian preacher quote verse 11!

> "Do you refuse to speak to me?" Pilate said. "Don't you realize I have power either to free you or to crucify you?"
>
> Jesus answered, "You would have no power over me if it were not given to you from above. Therefore the one who handed me over to you is guilty of a greater sin" (John 19:10-11).

It is true that God one time put his son into the hands of sinners; however, it is also true that these sinners shouted, "Crucify him! Crucify him!" (John 19:6b). Men put Christ to death but God raised him from the grave and gave him all power and authority. Christ also was given a new name (cf.

Philip. 2:9-11). The Father made his Son to be Lord. The real question is not what sinners will do with Christ, but the question is what will Jesus do with the sinner? He is not in our hands; we are in his hands. All men are in the hands of God's appointed Redeemer to do with as he chooses. Romans 1:1-4 helps us understand this point.

Paul, a servant of Jesus Christ, called to be an apostle, separated unto the gospel of God, (Which he had promised afore by his prophets in the holy scriptures,) Concerning his Son Jesus Christ our Lord, which was made of the seed of David according to the flesh; And declared to be the Son of God with power, according to the spirit of holiness, by the resurrection from the dead: (KJV).

John Murray's comments on Romans 1:1-4 are most helpful.

By his resurrection and ascension the Son of God incarnate entered upon a new phase of sovereignty and was endowed with new power correspondent with and unto the exercise of the mediatorial lordship which he executes as head over all things to his body, the church. [50]

In no sense whatsoever is Murray suggesting that Christ is more sovereign after the resurrection and ascension than he was before. Nor is he saying that finishing the redemptive work his father gave him added anything to his person. He is talking about the redemptive authority the man, Christ Jesus, earned in sufferings. The NIV in its translation of Romans 1:4, as it often does, gives an interpretation of the text instead of an accurate translation. Notice the difference between the KJV and the NIV:

Romans 1:4-KJV

---

[50] John Murray, *New International Commentary on the Testament, The Epistle to the Romans,* Vol. 1 (Grand Rapids, MI: Wm. Eerdman's Publishing Co., 1965), 11.

And declared to be the Son of God WITH POWER, according to the spirit of holiness, by the resurrection from the dead:

Romans 1:4-NIV

And who through the Spirit of holiness was DECLARED WITH POWER to be the Son of God by his resurrection from the dead: Jesus Christ our Lord.

As you can see, the NIV makes the resurrection to be a powerful demonstration of Christ's deity, and the KJV sees the resurrection as giving Christ a new and earned power or authority. The resurrection of Christ certainly is a "powerful demonstration" that "proves" the deity of Christ, but Paul in Romans 1:4 is not trying to prove that Christ was both human and deity. I grant that is the most common interpretation, but I think it totally misses the point taught in the text. Paul is saying that the resurrection declares that Christ has been given a power of Lordship as a reward for his successful atoning work. This is a redemptive Lordship that belongs to the Son of Mary as the successful Redeemer. It is not an innate Lordship that belongs to the Son of God as a member of the Trinity.

The man Christ Jesus is declared to be "Son of God with power because he is glorified and enthroned humanity. A true man, the God-Man, has been given the right to exercise both the role of Savior and the role of judge over all men. This Man earned that right. This truth is seen every time the "man Christ Jesus" is mentioned in the New Testament Scriptures. Note the following examples:

"Look," he said, "I see heaven open and the Son of Man standing at the right hand of God" (Acts 7:56).

"Therefore, my brothers, I want you to know that through Jesus the forgiveness of sins is proclaimed to you (Acts 13:38).

For he has set a day when he will judge the world with justice by the man he has appointed. He has given proof of this to all men by raising him from the dead" (Acts 17:31).

For there is one God and one mediator between God and men, the man Christ Jesus (1 Tim. 2:5).

Jesus has been found worthy of greater honor than Moses, just as the builder of a house has greater honor than the house itself (Heb. 3:3).

but because Jesus lives forever, he has a permanent priesthood. Therefore he is able to save completely those who come to God through him, because he always lives [as a true man] *to intercede for them* (Heb. 7:24-25).

This fact explains why the sermons in the Book of Acts emphasize both the resurrection and ascension of Christ. It is those events that prove Christ has been given a new authority.

"Men of Israel, listen to this: Jesus of Nazareth was a man accredited by God to you by miracles, wonders and signs, which God did among you through him, as you yourselves know. This man was handed over to you by God's set purpose and foreknowledge; and you, with the help of wicked men, put him to death by nailing him to the cross. But God raised him from the dead, freeing him from the agony of death, because it was impossible for death to keep its hold on him" (Acts 2:22-24).

The point of this passage is the resurrection, but Peter does not stop with just the resurrection. The heart of his sermon is verses 30-32.

But he was a prophet and knew that God had promised him on oath that he would place one of his descendants on his throne. Seeing what was ahead, he spoke of the resurrection of the Christ, that he was not abandoned to the grave, nor did his body see decay. God has raised this Jesus to life, and we are all witnesses of the fact (Acts 2:30-32).

The application of the sermon is in verses 33-36.

Exalted to the right hand of God, he has received from the Father the promised Holy Spirit and has poured out what you now see and hear. For David did not ascend to heaven, and yet he said, "'The Lord said to my Lord:

"Sit at my right hand
until I make your enemies
a footstool for your feet."'
"Therefore let all Israel be assured of this: God has made this Jesus,
whom you crucified, both Lord and Christ" (Acts 2:33-36).

There was a point in time when God the Father made Christ to be both Lord and Christ in a new sense. When did that happen? It took place at the resurrection and ascension. What is the peculiar authority that the Father gave the Son when he made him Lord over all flesh? The Father gave the Son the legal authority of Lordship to forgive and justify sinners. The ascension to the throne at the Father's right hand gave the man Christ Jesus the mediatorial rights to dispense the gifts he earned by his obedient life and vicarious death. The message of the Gospel to be preached is, "Therefore let all Israel be assured of this: God has made this Jesus, whom you crucified, both Lord and Christ." The man Christ Jesus, Son of God and son of Mary, is the judge of all men, and he is the Messiah who saves the sheep his Father gave him.

What must poor sinners do to be saved? They must bow in repentance and faith to the exalted Christ of God.

When the people heard this, they were cut to the heart and said to Peter and the other apostles, "Brothers, what shall we do?"

Peter replied, "Repent and be baptized, every one of you, in the name of Jesus Christ for the forgiveness of your sins. And you will receive the gift of the Holy Spirit. The promise is for you and your children and for all who are far off—for all whom the Lord our God will call."

With many other words he warned them; and he pleaded with them, "Save yourselves from this corrupt generation." Those who accepted his message were baptized, and about three thousand were added to their number that day.

They devoted themselves to the apostles' teaching and to the fellowship, to the breaking of bread and to prayer. Everyone was filled with awe, and many wonders and miraculous signs were done by the apostles. All the believers were together and had everything in common. Selling their possessions and goods, they gave to anyone as he had need. Every day they continued to meet together in the temple courts. They broke bread in their homes and ate together with glad and sincere hearts, praising God and enjoying the favor of all the people. And the Lord added to their number daily those who were being saved (Acts 2:37-47).

What is God's controversy with the people living in your town? The following quotation is taken from my booklet, *Christ, Lord and Lawgiver over the Church.*

The first denial [of the Lordship of Christ] is seen in *The Diluted Evangelistic Message Preached Today.* We clearly see Christ's Lordship denied when we see him preached as anything less than Lord. To imply that a sinner may receive Christ as anyone less than an enthroned Lord is equal to denying that he is Lord. Making salvation to be anything less than full and grateful submission to Christ as Lord, as well as Savior, is as wrong as denying that He rose from the dead and ascended into heaven. The present day controversy arising from John MacArthur's book entitled *The Gospel According To Jesus* is more than a discussion on how to preach. The bottom line is the person, dignity, and authority of Jesus Christ as Lord. Who is the person that we tell sinners to look to alone for salvation? What kind of salvation is freely offered to sinners by this Person? Dare we say to a sinner, "Jesus Christ is Lord, and he alone can save you. However, you really need not actually treat him as Lord in order to trust him as your Savior?" I honestly wish I were caricaturing, but you know I am not.

It is essential that we keep the focus on "who He is" and on "what He did." We need only look at the way Christ was proclaimed by the early church to prove our point. When Christ was born, His Lordship was emphasized: "For unto you is born this day in the city of David a Savior, which is Christ the LORD" (Luke 2:11). It is true that Christ is here presented as a Savior, but the message declared that he could be the Savior only because he was the Lord. Christ's Lordship cannot be separated from his Saviorhood. To even imply that a sinner can trust Christ as Savior and deny him as Lord is equally as bad as saying a sinner can trust Christ as his Lord and, at the same time, ridicule and mock his priestly work of blood atonement. We must declare a Savior who is the Lord, or we are denying his Lordship. This is surely the pattern in the entire New Testament Scriptures: "Believe on the LORD Jesus Christ...Therefore let all the house of Israel know assuredly, that God hath made the same Jesus, whom ye have crucified, both LORD and Christ...if thou shalt confess with thy mouth the LORD Jesus" (or "that Jesus is Lord") (Acts 16:31; 2:36; Rom. 10:9). [51]

The Gospel presents a whole Savior. He is Prophet, Priest and King. We insist the Gospel affects the whole man, mind, heart and will. Nowhere in the New Testament Scriptures are sinners told to "accept Jesus as your personal Savior." That phrase enshrines the totality of modern orthodox theology. We could just as well say, "Accept Jesus as your personal Priest or accept Jesus as your personal King." The emphasis is never on the office but on trusting the person who holds the office, and that person is always the Lord Jesus Christ. God's salvation is in a living Lord, and we receive him in all his fullness and not merely his offices or his benefits. Bowing in repentance and faith to the risen and enthroned Lord is the gospel message of the early church.

This emphasis on Lordship does not end with the sinner's conversion. Holiness and following after Christ were also couched in terms of Lordship: "So then, just as you received Christ Jesus as Lord, continue to live in him," (Col. 2:6). Notice that believers were urged to follow Christ as Lord because they had received him in conversion as Lord. There is no other kind of gospel or conversion.

---

[51] Reisinger, *Christ, Lord and Lawgiver*, 7.

Someday every person who has ever lived will acknowledge Jesus Christ as Lord.

> *Therefore God exalted him to the highest place*
> *and gave him the name that is above every name,*
>
> *that at the name of Jesus every knee should bow,*
> *in heaven and on earth and under the earth,*
>
> *and every tongue confess that Jesus Christ is Lord,*
> *to the glory of God the Father* (Philip. 2:9-11).

The new name given to Christ at the resurrection is not "Jesus;" that is the human name given to him at his birth. Mary was told to call her unborn son Jesus—"... and you are to give him the name Jesus ..." (Matt. 1:21). The new name given to him as a reward for his redemptive work is "Lord." That is the name he earned and which was given to him by his Father at the resurrection.

God's controversy with sinners is not merely their refusal to mentally believe that Christ was really born of a virgin. Nearly our whole society confesses that fact at Christmas time. Roman Catholics have built their whole pagan system of Maryology on a gross misuse of that truth. Nor is God's controversy with sinners their refusal to accept by faith that Christ rose from dead. Again, our churches will be packed on Easter Sunday with people confessing they believe the resurrection of Christ actually took place.

What then is God's controversy with sinners? What is his controversy with the people in your city? It has nothing to do with faith, as a mental assent, in the historic reality of the birth, death and resurrection of Christ. I repeat, Christmas and Easter give ample proof of such faith. God's controversy with sinners is their refusal to bow in repentance and faith to the one who God has made to be Lord. It is the rejection of the Lordship of Christ over their life that is the sinner's problem, and we are called to face sinners with that problem by pressing the claims of Jesus Christ as Lord. We must demand that the sinner lay down the weapons of his warfare and rebellion and totally and unconditionally surrender to a gracious King.

God the Father says that Jesus is Lord. What say ye?

Christie,
Our Ascended King
Chapter 13

It may be helpful to review some comments we made in the introduction to this study on "Christ, Our New Covenant Prophet, Priest and King." The Old Testament Scriptures set forth Moses, Aaron (and Melchizedek) and David as types of Christ in his work as Prophet, Priest and King. In each case, the New Testament Scriptures demonstrate exactly how Christ fulfills all three of these offices.

One, Christ is "that Prophet" who fulfills the promise God made to Moses in Deuteronomy 18:15. "The LORD your God will raise up for you a prophet like me from among your own brothers. You must listen to him."

Two, Christ is the "Priest after the order of Melchizedek" as promised in Psalm 110:4. "The LORD has sworn and will not change his mind: 'You are a priest forever, in the order of Melchizedek.'" Christ is also the high priest who replaces Aaron and the Levitical priesthood.

Three, Christ is David's greater Son who established the everlasting kingdom promised to David and now sits on the throne in fulfillment of the Davidic covenant made in 2 Samuel 7:12, 13. "When your days are over and you rest with your fathers, I will raise up your offspring to succeed you, who will come from your own body, and I will establish his kingdom. He is the one who will build a house for my Name, and I will establish the throne of his kingdom forever."

The Holy Spirit, in the New Testament Scriptures, used powerful object lessons to show, in each case, how Christ is the fulfillment of all three of these types.

1) The Mount of Transfiguration (Matt.17:1-6) is the object lesson that shows the new Prophet has replaced Moses as Prophet and Lawgiver. The new Prophet also replaced all of the old covenant prophets as God's spokesmen. The message from heaven saying, "Listen to my Son" is the Father showing the change from the old authority to the new and final authority. This is the same message proclaimed in the Book of Hebrews (1:1-3). Christ is the last and final prophet. He has given us the full and final message of God. God has said all he has to say in his Son.

2) The rending of the veil of the Temple from top to bottom at the moment of Christ's death (Matt. 27:50-51) is the object lesson showing that the new Priest has replaced Aaron and fulfilled the Melchizedek prophecy. Again, this message is explicit in Hebrews (9:1-10; 10:19-22). The message of, "… have confidence to enter the Most Holy Place by the blood of Jesus, by a new and living way opened for us through the curtain, that is, his body,"(Heb. 10:19, 20) could never have been preached as long as the Levitical priesthood was in effect and the veil in the temple was hanging in place.

3) The gift of tongues on the Day of Pentecost (Acts 2:1- 36) is the object lesson showing that the resurrection and ascension of Christ to sit on the throne of David has established the kingdom promised to David and prophesied in both Joel 2 and 2 Samuel 7. The message is bow in repentance, faith and assurance before the newly crowned King (cf. Philip. 2:5-8), or as the Psalmist said, "Kiss the Son" (Psalm 2:12).

It is easy to see in Matthew 17:1-6, the Mount of Transfiguration, the object lesson showing Christ being established as our New Covenant Prophet. It is also easy to see in Matthew

27:50-51, the rending of the veil, Christ's work as our New Covenant High Priest. However, seeing the events recorded on the Day of Pentecost as an object lesson showing the coronation of Christ as our New Covenant King is not quite as obvious. How does speaking in tongues demonstrate the kingship of Christ? The primary problem is a failure to understand the theological significance of what really happened on the day of Pentecost. On the day of Pentecost, as recorded in Acts 2, bewildered people asked this question: "What does this mean? What is going on?" They were surely asking the right question. The short answer is, the gift of tongues was the evidence that the Holy Spirit had come in fulfillment of the prophecy in Joel concerning the promise of the kingdom and the coming of the Holy Spirit, and that in turn proved that Christ had ascended to heaven and was seated on David's promised throne as King as promised to David in 2 Samuel 7. Christ alone could send the Spirit. He earned that right in his redemptive work.

There are three passages of Scripture that teach us how we are to understand the significance of speaking in tongues. The first is Genesis 11; the second is Acts 2; and the third is 1 Corinthians 14. Genesis 11 records the beginning of tongues and the purpose for which they were given. Acts 2 records the second giving of tongues on the Day of Pentecost. 1 Corinthians 14 gives the new covenant meaning and the purpose of tongues. If we don't understand the message that God was teaching on the day of Pentecost, we will never understand the meaning and significance of speaking in tongues.

If a person understood the biblical meaning of speaking in tongues, I doubt he would be very inclined to seek that experience. I have often said that, (1) "If Scripture commands me to seek the gift of speaking in tongues, I have no choice but to start seeking that gift. So far I have not seen such a commandment in Scripture. (2) If speaking in tongues would help me in my Christian life or help me in my ministry as a pastor, again, I would be biblically obligated to start seeking. Again, I find no such idea in Scripture. Let's digress for a moment and make sure we understand the meaning of speaking in tongues.

There is no question that tongues were given by God to be a sign. Paul explicitly says, "Tongues, then, are a sign," (1 Cor. 14:22). With such a clear statement, everyone must agree that tongues were given by God to be a sign; however, there is not much agreement as to what the tongues signify. The problem is not a lack of clarity in the Scripture. The place to start a study of tongues is the first time tongues are mentioned in Scripture, namely, in Genesis 11. I do not know why this is so rarely done. We have a lot of unanswered questions in this passage, but several things are clear. First, the desire of the people to build a city "with a tower that reaches to the heavens" was born out of rebellion to God (cf. Gen. 11:4-6). Second, prior to Genesis 11 everyone spoke the same language. When they set out to build a tower to reach to heaven, God deliberately confused their language, so they could not understand each other. Third, it is clear in this passage, and just as it is clear in 1 Corinthians 14 and Acts 2, that speaking in tongues is an evidence of the judgment of God. The existence of tongues is the evidence of disobedience to God being punished. That is clear from Genesis 11 as well as the specific statement in 1 Corinthians 14:21-22 quoting Isaiah 28:11-12.

Here is the first mention of tongues in Scripture.

Now the whole world had one language and a common speech. As men moved eastward, they found a plain in Shinar and settled there.

They said to each other, "Come, let's make bricks and bake them thoroughly." They used brick instead of stone, and tar for mortar. Then they said, "Come, let us build ourselves a city, with a tower that reaches to the heavens, so that we may make a name for ourselves and not be scattered over the face of the whole earth."

But the Lord came down to see the city and the tower that the men were building. The Lord said, "If as one people speaking the same language they have begun to do this, then nothing they plan to do will be impossible for them. Come, let us go down and confuse their language so they will not understand each other."

So the Lord scattered them from there over all the earth, and they stopped building the city. That is why it was called Babel—because there the Lord confused the language of the whole world. From there the Lord scattered them over the face of the whole earth (Gen. 11:1-9).

These verses describe both the origin of tongues and God's purpose in creating the multiplicity of tongues. One thing is clear. Speaking in different tongues was an evidence of God's judgment. We will first look at Acts 2 and then look at Paul's interpretation of the meaning of the amazing events that took place on the day of Pentecost and its relationship to Passover and the Day of Atonement.

When the day of Pentecost came, they were all together in one place. Suddenly a sound like the blowing of a violent wind came from heaven and filled the whole house where they were sitting. They saw what seemed to be tongues of fire that separated and came to rest on each of them. All of them were filled with the Holy Spirit and began to speak in other tongues as the Spirit enabled them (Acts 2:1-4).

Exactly when did the Holy Spirit come and empower the speaking in tongues? When did the day of Pentecost come? Did the Holy Spirit come before or after the speaking in tongues recorded in Acts 2? These are both simple and vital questions, but they are usually ignored. Acts 2:1 is quite clear. The events recorded in Acts 2 took place after the Day of Pentecost had already come! Scripture says, "When the day of Pentecost came," or, as the KJV translates it, "When the day of Pentecost was fully come." Listen very carefully. The day the Holy Spirit came and the miracle of tongues took place is not called the "day of Pentecost" because the Holy Spirit came on that day. The Holy Spirit came on that day because it was already the day of Pentecost. It was the only day the Spirit could have come! The speaking in tongues was the proof that the day of Pentecost had come. It was not the day of Pentecost because the Holy Spirit came that day. The Holy Spirit had to come fifty days after the Feast of Passover. Look carefully at verse 1. "When the day of Pentecost came." The things recorded in Acts 2:2-4 took place after the day of Pentecost had come. It was already the day of Pentecost when the Holy Spirit came. The tongues were the sign or proof that Christ had ascended to heaven, been seated on his throne at the Father's hand, and had sent the Holy Spirit to be his vicar on earth.

The Holy Spirit came on the day of Pentecost because he was scheduled to come on that day. Leviticus 23 records the various Jewish feast days. The seventh day Sabbath heads the list of feast days (Lev. 23:3). Next on the list is the feast of Passover. In Leviticus 23:5 Passover is explained. Our Lord died on Passover day. He was the true Passover lamb. In Leviticus 23:15-16, the Feast of First Fruits is explained. This feast is to be observed fifty days after Passover. It was also called the Feast of Pentecost since the word *pente* means fifty. The Holy Spirit came on the day of Pentecost, fifty days after Passover, for the same reason that Christ died on Passover day. Both Passover and Pentecost were prophesied in Leviticus 23, and Pentecost was clearly scheduled to occur fifty days after the feast of Passover. Pentecost was the only day that Holy Spirit could have come just as Passover was the only day upon which Christ could die on the cross. None of the events that happened on any feast day had anything to do with either naming or performing the event. Each feast day defined the events and the time they were to be observed. It was all clearly prophesied and fulfilled down to the slightest detail.

The idea that the early church 'prayed down the Holy Spirit' and we can pray down another Pentecost today is nonsense. The Holy Spirit came right on schedule just as Christ died right on schedule. There can never be another day of Pentecost without there also being another Passover lamb offered as our sin bearer. There can be no more days of Pentecost unless there is another Day of Atonement. There cannot be another day of Pentecost unless it is preceded by Christ dying on the cross fifty days earlier.

Acts 2:4 says they spoke in tongues "as the Spirit enabled them." This may mean that all those gathered did not speak in tongues. Verses 12 and 13 are clear that all who were present did not hear the Gospel message being preached. Some heard only incoherent babbling. Part of the miracle may have been on the ear of the listener as well as the tongue of the speaker.

Verses 5-8 state that they were "utterly amazed" because they heard in their own languages (16 different Gentile Languages). This proves that the tongues spoken on the day of Pentecost were known languages. As we shall see, this is also one of the key facts in understanding the meaning of tongues.

> Now there were staying in Jerusalem God-fearing Jews from every nation under heaven. When they heard this sound, a crowd came together in bewilderment, because each one heard their own language being spoken. Utterly amazed, they asked: "Aren't all these who are speaking Galileans? Then how is it that each of us hears them in our native language? (Acts 2:5-8).

Verses 11–13 again say that they were all "amazed," but this second amazement was because of what they heard. It was not merely hearing in their own language, but it was the content of the message that they heard that amazed them. Verse 11 says they heard the "wonders of God in [their] own tongues!" They heard the Gospel. However, they were amazed because they were hearing the "wonders of God" not in the sacred Hebrew language but in Gentiles' languages. This is the heart of the message of the miraculous sign of tongues. As we shall see, God speaking the gospel in Gentile languages instead of the sacred Hebrew language was a deliberate rebuke by God and signaled that God was turning from the Jews to the Gentiles. The Jews heard the gospel in Gentile languages. They were not drunk, but they were confused. They were witnessing the unthinkable. God was showing grace to the Gentiles and was giving the Gentiles the same privileges as the Jews.

> *... we hear them declaring the wonders of God in our own tongues!" Amazed and perplexed, they asked one another, "What does this mean?" Some, however, made fun of them and said, "They have had too much wine"* (Acts 2:11-13).

In Verses 14-16 Peter insists that the apostles were not drunk. He first declares that the things taking place were the fulfillment of the prophecy in the Book of Joel. The promised kingdom in Joel had come, and the events of Pentecost were a clear proof that Christ had been exalted to the Father's right hand. Our Lord is the promised greater son of David being declared King. The promise in Joel concerned a universal gospel not just a Jewish gospel. The kingdom promised in Joel was for "all nations" not just the nation of Israel.

> *Then Peter stood up with the Eleven, raised his voice and addressed the crowd: "Fellow Jews and all of you who live in Jerusalem, let me explain this to you; listen carefully to what I say. These people are not drunk, as you suppose. It's only nine in the morning! No, this is what was spoken by the prophet Joel:"* (Acts 2:14-16).

Verse 16 is a key passage. It shows us how the New Testament writers interpret kingdom prophecy. When Peter says "this is what was spoken" he is clearly spiritualizing Joel's prophecy. Dispensationalism must insist this is only a type, a preview or foreshadowing of Joel's prophecy. They insist, "The Holy Spirit has not yet been "poured out on all flesh" as

promised in Joel. The prophecy in Joel has not yet been fulfilled. It will not be literally fulfilled until the earthly millennium has been established. John MacArthur gives the dispensational view in his study Bible.

> Joel's prophecy will not be completely fulfilled until the mil-
> lennial kingdom and the final judgment. But Peter, by using it
> shows that Pentecost was a pre-fulfillment, a taste of what will
> happen in the millennial kingdom when the Spirit is poured
> out on all flesh (cf. 10:45). [52]

Regardless of your prophetic view, the essence of Joel's
prophecy and Peter's sermon is verse 21. The Gospel is now
to be preached to the whole world and not just to Jews. It is
no longer to the Jew first and also to the Gentile but it is *whosoever*. That was what Joel prophesied, and that is what Peter
preached as the fulfillment of Joel's prophecy. Look up the
exact prophecy in Joel that Peter is quoting as being fulfilled
at Pentecost.

> *And afterward, I will pour out my Spirit on all people. Your sons
> and daughters will prophesy, your old men will dream dreams, your
> young men will see visions.*
>
> *Even on my servants, both men and women, I will pour out my
> Spirit in those days. I will show wonders in the heavens and on the
> earth, blood and fire and billows of smoke. The sun will be turned to
> darkness and the moon to blood before the coming of the great and
> dreadful day of the LORD. And everyone who calls on the name of the
> LORD will be saved; for on Mount Zion and in Jerusalem there will be
> deliverance, as the LORD has said, among the survivors whom the
> LORD calls* (Joel 2:28-32).

Verse 28 emphasizes that the pouring out of the Holy Spirit
will be "on all people," Jews and Gentiles alike, and not just
the Jews. Verses 28 and 29 speak of all ages, young and old,

---

[52] John MacArthur, *The MacArthur Study Bible* (Word Publishing, 1997),
1635.

and without respect of gender. Normally old men quit dreaming, and young men have no vision of tomorrow and think only of today. When the Holy Spirit moves in a congregation, the old men get out of their rocking chairs and say, "Let's go." They begin to act like their great grandpa Caleb. The young men begin to see eternity and start to prioritize their life accordingly. This double phenomenon is a mark of the presence of the Holy Spirit at work in a congregation.

Verses 30 and 31 are spiritualized by Peter in Acts 2:19-20. Those who demand a "literal" interpretation of kingdom prophecy insist that the Joel prophecy has not yet been literally fulfilled. Do they believe the moon must be literally turned into a giant blob of blood before this prophecy is fulfilled? The question is not must we spiritualize the Joel passage but how much of it we must spiritualize. Even more importantly we must ask, "How does Peter understand the prophecy of Joel?" Does "this is what was spoken" really mean what it says? Dare we literalize what Peter explicitly spiritualizes? Regardless of your view of prophecy, Peter distinctly says, "… this is what was spoken by the prophet Joel:" It sounds to me like Peter is definitely saying Joel's prophecy is being fulfilled on the day of Pentecost.

The application of the whole prophecy and its importance for us today is verse 32.

> And everyone who calls on the name of the LORD will be saved; for on Mount Zion and in Jerusalem there will be deliverance, as the LORD has said, among the survivors whom the LORD calls (Joel 2:32).

The day of Pentecost established the fact that the Gospel was now a 'whosoever Gospel for the whole world' and not just for the Jews. Peter shows that Joel was talking about salvation in the Gospel age not a future earthly millennia age. Joel is in effect saying, "A deliverer [Christ the Messiah] is coming who will bring full deliverance [salvation] to the elect of God from every tongue and nation." Peter is saying, "That deliverer has come and fulfilled this promise." David's son has established the kingdom and sits on the heavenly throne as king. The phrase "among the survivors whom the LORD calls" is shown in Acts 2:39 to mean the elect from all nations. Notice how Peter understood the words of Joel's prophecy.

First, Acts 2:14-21 is the apostolic interpretation of Joel's prophecy concerning the promised kingdom.

Second, Acts 2:22-36 is the apostolic interpretation of (1) God's promise to David to raise up one of his sons to sit on his throne and establish his kingdom (cf. 2 Sam. 7), and also (2) Joel's prophecy that Jesus was the Messiah who would establish the kingdom promised to Abraham and his spiritual descendants. The message by Peter is clear. Both the promise that Messiah would, (1) sit on David's throne as king, and (2), the kingdom promise of a universal Gospel of "whosoever," not just the Jews, has fully come. The day of Pentecost declaring the Gospel to all nations was proof that David's throne and kingdom are established and his Son is seated on that throne as King of King and Lord of Lords with all power and authority. The sending of the Holy Spirit by the enthroned Lord is the proof that the prophecies to both Joel and to David have been fulfilled.

Acts 2:38-40 are the conclusion of Peter's explanation of Pentecost.

> Peter replied, "Repent and be baptized, every one of you, in the name of Jesus Christ for the forgiveness of your sins. And you will receive the gift of the Holy Spirit. The promise is for you and your children and for all who are far off—for all whom the Lord our God will call."

> With many other words he warned them; and he pleaded with them, "Save yourselves from this corrupt generation."

Verse 38 declares that the gift of the Holy Spirit is the great Gospel blessing. The gift of the Holy Spirit was the great promise in the Old Testament Scriptures, and the actual receiving the indwelling Spirit as the Spirit of Adoption is the great experience of the new covenant. The point of Peter's sermon is that this prophecy in Joel concerning the Holy Spirit has been fulfilled, and the events of Pentecost are the proof.

We must remember that the Jews hated the message that "there is no longer any difference" between Jews and Gentiles. There was a great difference between Israel and the Gentiles under the old covenant. It was God Himself who made that difference; however, under the Gospel age, as promised in Joel, there is no longer Jew nor Greek, bond or free, etc., see Galatians 3:26-29.

It is even more important to remember that the great difference between Israelites and Gentiles was not that an Israelite was in a separate "spiritual" category. The Jewish child, like a child born into a Christian home, had great privileges (Rom. 3:1-3) but was not in a separate spiritual category. An unsaved Jew was just as lost as a Gentile and got converted the same way, namely, by believing the Gospel promise. The same is true today. A child born in a Christian home is just as lost, until they repent and believe the gospel, as a child of pagan parents.

Two things happened to the Jew/Gentile situation on the day of Pentecost when the Body of Christ, the new man of Ephesians and the new creation of 2 Corinthians 5:17, came into being through the baptism of the Holy Spirit. First, believing Gentiles were made equal with believing Jews. This is the "mystery" Paul spoke of in chapter 3 of Ephesians. The Old Testament Scriptures clearly saw Gentiles being saved but nowhere was a total equality of Jew and Gentile in the

Body of Christ foretold. All of that changed on the day of Pentecost. Second, unbelieving Jews were made equal to the Gentile dogs. This is laid out in Ephesians 2. Since the Cross and Pentecost "there is no difference."

We need to say a word about Romans 9:1-8. This section deals with Israel's special covenantal relationship with God. Paul's whole argument hinges on one point. The Jews had many and great privileges, but they were never in a saving covenantal relationship with God. They had privileges that the Gentiles did not have, but they were not in a special spiritual category. (See also Romans 3:1-2).

I speak the truth in Christ—I am not lying, my conscience confirms it in the Holy Spirit—I have great sorrow and unceasing anguish in my heart. For I could wish that I myself were cursed and cut off from Christ for the sake of my brothers, those of my own race, the people of Israel. Theirs is the adoption as sons; theirs the divine glory, the covenants, the receiving of the law, the temple worship and the promises. Theirs are the patriarchs, and from them is traced the human ancestry of Christ, who is God over all, forever praised! Amen.

It is not as though God's word had failed. For not all who are descended from Israel are Israel. Nor because they are his descendants are they all Abraham's children. On the contrary, "It is through Isaac that your offspring will be reckoned." In other words, it is not the natural children who are God's children, but it is the children of the promise who are regarded as Abraham's offspring (Rom. 9:1-8).

First of all, the context is important. Romans chapter 8 is the great chapter on assurance and hope. Paul goes from one level of assurance to another level like a great piece of music. He closes with that powerful statement that absolutely nothing can separate any person, who is in a saving covenant relationship with God, from God's love and acceptance.

Second, the obvious question is, "Paul, what about Israel? Were they not God's covenant people and were not some of them cast off?" It is true that some of Israel was cast off but that in no way proves God went back on his covenant promise. The short answer to this question is that "not all Israel is Israel." Israel was never in a saving covenant relationship with God whereby they were promised salvation because of either their birth or their circumcision. Romans 9:1-8 shows that Israel was never in a saving covenant relationship with God. They had many privileges but never took advantage of them. Hebrews 3 and 4 makes that very clear. Israel had the promise of the Gospel preached to them but did not believe that promise.

> Therefore, since the promise of entering his rest still stands, let us be careful that none of you be found to have fallen short of it. For we also have had the gospel preached to us, just as they did; but the message they heard was of no value to them, because those who heard did not combine it with faith (Heb. 4:1-2).

God has never promised anyone, either a Jew or anyone else, any spiritual blessing just because of either his or her birth or circumcision and irrespective of faith. God sovereignly gives some people far more privileges than others, but none of those privileges guarantee salvation.

Third, the comparison between "children of the flesh" and the "children of the promise" in Romans 9:8 is not a comparison between covenant and non-covenant children. The comparison is between covenant circumcised Israelites who are part of the elect and those covenant circumcised Israelites who were not elect. There were Jacobs and Esaus among the covenant people of Israel just as there are Jacobs and Esaus among the children of Christian parents. God's promise is with those who believe and has nothing to do with birth or baptism.

Christ,
Our New Covenant King
Chapter 14

Most agree with much of what we said earlier about Christ as our Prophet and Priest, but there is great disagreement concerning Christ in the role of King. The primary reason for the disagreement centers on dispensationalism's position on the establishing of a future earthly kingdom with one of David's sons sitting on the throne of that kingdom as king. This is referred to as "the Davidic kingdom."

Scripture is quite clear in 2 Samuel 7:1-17 and 1 Chronicles 17:1-15 that God promised David that he, God, would establish a future kingdom and raise up one of David's sons to sit as king on a throne in that kingdom. No one disputes the fact of that covenant. However, all do not agree on either the nature of the promised kingdom to David or the time of the promise being fulfilled. I insist that the kingdom promised to David was a spiritual kingdom that was established by Christ at his first coming. I believe Christ is already sitting on the throne of that kingdom. The kingdom promised to David is the Church and Christ is David's greater son. Classical dispensationalism disagrees and insists that the kingdom promised to David was an earthly kingdom, and it is not yet established. Jesus is said to have offered that kingdom to the Jews at his first coming, and they rejected it. It was postponed and will be fulfilled in a future earthly millennium. The following note in the first edition of the Scofield Bible sets forth classical dispensationalism's position on the Davidic kingdom and throne.

II. Four *forms* of the Gospel are to be distinguished:

(1) The Gospel of the kingdom. This is the good news that God purposes to set up on the earth, in fulfillment of the Davidic Covenant (2 Sam. vii. 8, and *refs.*), a kingdom, political, spiritual, Israelitish, universal, over which God's Son, David's heir, shall be King, and which shall be, for one thousand years, the manifestation of the righteousness of God in human affairs.[53]

Dispensationalism is clear that Christ is not yet reigning as king. These writers will often state that Christ is our Prophet, Priest and *coming* King. The following Scofield footnote defining the second "form of the Gospel" refers to Jesus as the "rejected king." It is the second of four forms of the Gospel.

(2) The Gospel of the grace of God. This is the good news that Jesus Christ, the *rejected* (italics added) King, has died on the cross for the sins of the world, that He was raised from the dead for our justification, and that by Him all that believe are justified from all things.[54]

I do not believe that it was a "rejected king" that died on the cross for my sins. I totally reject the statement, "Jesus Christ, the rejected King, has died on the cross." It was not a rejected king that died for me. This idea is a necessary consequence of holding the postponement theory. I believe the death of Christ on the cross is the good news that Jesus Christ, not a rejected king, but God's anointed Son and ordained Prophet, Priest and King, has, in perfect fulfillment of the eternal purpose and promise of the Father, died on the cross as promised and covenanted.

It is no accident that another consequence of rejecting the present kingship of Christ is the carnal Christian doctrine. Many modern dispensationalists reject the carnal Christian

---

[53] C.I. Scofield, editor, *The First Scofield Reference Bible* (Westwood, NJ: Barbour and Company, 1986), 1343.

[54] Ibid.

doctrine, but others say such people are inconsistent in so doing. I am sure it is not intended, but Scofield in the above quotation makes the cross sound like a "plan B" or after-thought. God's real purpose and goal, or plan A, was establishing the earthly kingdom, but the Jews refused to go along with that so plan B, the cross and the Church, was put into effect. Plan A was "postponed" until the second coming of Christ. The nature of the kingdom and its supposed rejection and postponement is at the heart of the theology of dispensationalism. It seems to me this downgrades the cross even though that was certainly not its intention.

It might be well to mention several things that are often not discussed when dispensationalism is taught. For instance, the footnote just quoted defines the kingdom promised to David as being "political, spiritual, Israelitish, universal, over which God's Son, David's heir, shall reign as King." If Jesus would have offered the Jews a kingdom that was "political, spiritual, Israelitish and universal," they would have accepted it without hesitation. They would never have crucified him. They would have shouted, "Amen!" Those words, especially the word Israeltitish, perfectly describe the very kind of kingdom the Jews wanted. Another point established in the quotation is that this covenant made with David has not yet been fulfilled. It will be fulfilled when the millennium is supposedly to be established. The New Testament makes it clear the Davidic kingdom is already established.

The whole subject of an earthly kingdom would be much easier to understand if we remembered one clear fact. The whole idea of an earthly kingdom and king to rule over Israel was born out of Israel's rebellion to God. The first mention of an earthly kingdom is found in 1 Samuel 8. Israel insisted they wanted to be like the other nations and have a king. Their desire for a king was a deliberate rejection of God as their king.

So all the elders of Israel gathered together and came to Samuel at Ramah. They said to him, "You are old, and your sons do not follow your ways; now appoint a king to lead us, such as all the other nations have." But when they said, "Give us a king to lead us," this displeased Samuel; so he prayed to the Lord. And the Lord told him: "Listen to all that the people are saying to you; it is not you they have rejected, but they have rejected me as their king (1 Sam. 8:4-7).

God instructed Samuel to warn the Israelites of the demands that a king would make of them and told them that they would be sorry for rejecting him as their king.

As they have done from the day I brought them up out of Egypt until this day, forsaking me and serving other gods, so they are doing to you. Now listen to them; but warn them solemnly and let them know what the king who will reign over them will claim as his rights." Samuel told all the words of the Lord to the people who were asking him for a king. He said, "This is what the king who will reign over you will claim as his rights: He will take your sons and make them serve with his chariots and horses, and they will run in front of his chariots. Some he will assign to be commanders of thousands and commanders of fifties, and others to plow his ground and reap his harvest, and still others to make weapons of war and equipment for his chariots. He will take your daughters to be perfumers and cooks and bakers. He will take the best of your fields and vineyards and olive groves and give them to his attendants. He will take a tenth of your grain and of your vintage and give it to his officials and attendants. Your male and female servants and the best of your cattle and donkeys he will take for his own use. He will take a tenth of your flocks, and you yourselves will become his slaves. When that day comes, you will cry out for relief from the king you have chosen, but the Lord will not answer you in that day" (1 Sam. 8:8-18).

The people refused to heed God's warning but insisted that they wanted a king. They wanted to be like all the other nations. They chose Saul as their king and suffered the disastrous results. Regardless of what millennial view you hold it must take into account the fact that an earthly king over God's people in an earthly kingdom "like the other nations" was born out of Israel's conscious and deliberate rejection of God as their king. There is no mention or intimation that God desired an earthly king to be established. The idea totally originated in Israel's rejection of God as their king.

> *But the people refused to listen to Samuel. "No!" they said. "We want a king over us. Then we will be like all the other nations, with a king to lead us and to go out before us and fight our battles." When Samuel heard all that the people said, he repeated it before the Lord. The Lord answered, "Listen to them and give them a king"* (1 Sam. 8:19-22).

In 1 Samuel 12, Samuel recounts some of Israel's history and reminds them of their rash decision to reject God as their king and choose an earthly king to rule over them, "… you said to me, 'No, we want a king to rule over us'–even though the Lord your God was your king" (v 12). It seems to me that any doctrine that has its origins in man's rebellion should at least make us tread lightly. We surely should not use something born out of rebellion to God as the foundation points of an important doctrine.

I am sure that many of my readers would like to ask, "Why would God deliberately allow Israel to choose an earthly king and reject him as their king." I cannot answer that question—nor can anyone else. We may speculate and come up with some very plausible reasons, but they would all be mere speculation. We face two dangers in seeking to understand Scripture. One, we need the courage to follow Scripture as far as it goes on any subject. We must not either avoid or minimize anything Scripture says. Many sincere people feel a subject should be avoided if it is controversial. That is saying that God put something in Scripture that should not be there. If God put something in Scripture, we must seek to understand it. Two, we need the humility to stop where God stops. Hyper-Calvinism uses human logic to deduce more than Scripture actually says. John Calvin emphasized this need for humility when discussing predestination. He said we must admit to having a "learned ignorance." Logic is a wonderful handmaid but a hard master. Logic cannot deduce truth that is not stated in actual texts of Scripture. It is just as arrogant to add our human wisdom to Scripture as it is to detract from Scripture.

The kingship of David begins with his secret anointing by Samuel as recorded in 1 Samuel 16. That is an interesting passage. God instructs Samuel to anoint one of Jesse the Bethelemite's sons as king. Samuel assumes it would be Eliab, the oldest son. Samuel thought, "Surely, the Lord's anointed stands here … " but God said no and then gave Samuel a lesson on choosing leadership.

"… Do not consider his appearance or his height, for I have rejected him. The Lord does not look at the things people look at. People look at the outward appearance, but the Lord looks at the heart"
(1 Sam. 16:7).

You would think that Israel would have learned the folly of judging by outward appearance. Saul won the beauty contest by unanimous vote, but he was a dud. He was not God's man. Jesse brought in every son until only David was left and each time God said no. Jesse did not even bring David in. Samuel had to ask, "Are these all the sons you have?" (1 Sam. 16:11). Then David was brought in and God told Samuel, "Rise and anoint him; he is the one" (1 Sam. 16:12).

It will be a long and tumultuous time before David is anointed king by all of Israel. After Saul's death he will be anointed by the tribe of Judah (2 Sam. 2) and later by all 12 tribes (2 Sam. 5).

The next important event in David's kingship is God making a covenant with David. It is recorded in 2 Samuel 7 and 1 Chronicles 17. David has been anointed king over all Israel.

He wants to build a house for God to dwell in. He shares his desire with Nathan the prophet and Nathan says, "Go ahead, God is with you." That night God told Nathan that he did not want David to build him a house. God then promises to build a house for David. That house is the Church and David's greater son who will build the house is Christ. That is not speculation on my part; it is quoting the New Testament interpretation of the Davidic covenant.

After the king was settled in his palace and the Lord had given him rest from all his enemies around him, he said to Nathan the prophet, "Here I am, living in a palace of cedar, while the ark of God remains in a tent."

Nathan replied to the king, "Whatever you have in mind, go ahead and do it, for the Lord is with you."

That night the word of the Lord came to Nathan, saying:

"Go and tell my servant David, 'This is what the Lord says: Are you the one to build me a house to dwell in? I have not dwelt in a house from the day I brought the Israelites up out of Egypt to this day. I have been moving from place to place with a tent as my dwelling. Wherever I have moved with all the Israelites, did I ever say to any of their rulers whom I commanded to shepherd my people Israel, "Why have you not built me a house of cedar?"'

"Now then, tell my servant David, 'This is what the Lord Almighty says: I took you from the pasture and from following the flock to be ruler over my people Israel. I have been with you wherever you have gone, and I have cut off all your enemies from before you. Now I will make your name great, like the names of the greatest men of the earth. And I will provide a place for my people Israel and will plant them so that they can have a home of their own and no longer be disturbed. Wicked people will not oppress them anymore, as they did at the beginning and have done ever since the time I appointed leaders over my people Israel. I will also give you rest from all your enemies.

"'The Lord declares to you that the Lord himself will establish a house for you: When your days are over and you rest with your fathers, I will raise up your offspring to succeed you, who will come

*from your own body, and I will establish his kingdom. He is the one
who will build a house for my Name, and I will establish the throne of
his kingdom forever. I will be his father, and he will be my son. When
he does wrong, I will punish him with the rod of men, with floggings
inflicted by men. But my love will never be taken away from him, as I
took it away from Saul, whom I removed from before you. Your house
and your kingdom will endure forever before me; your throne will be
established forever.'"*

Nathan reported to David all the words of this entire revelation (2
Sam. 7:1-17).

The heart of God's covenant with David is found in verse
13, "He is the one who will build a house for my Name, and I
will establish the throne of his kingdom forever." Hebrews
3:6 specifically calls the Church God's house, "But Christ is
faithful as a son over God's house. We are his house, ..." Believers are the true and final temple of God in which God
dwells. We are the true house of David. Christ is David's
greater son and is building the true house of God out of living
stones. Again, this is not speculation; it is quoting the New
Testament. In 2 Samuel 7:12 part of the promise to David was
that God would "... raise up your offspring to succeed you,
who will come from your own body, ..." When Peter quotes
that text in Acts 2:30, he changes the word "seed" to the word
"Christ," "...he would raise up Christ (David's seed) to sit on
his throne." Look at the two texts.

*When your days are over and you rest with your fathers, I will
raise up your offspring ["seed" – KJV] to succeed you, ...* (2 Sam.
7:12)

*Therefore, being a prophet, and knowing that God had sworn with
an oath to him that of the fruit of his body, according to the flesh, He
would raise up the Christ to sit on his throne* (Acts 2:30 NKJV).

David understood that God was talking about Christ. David also understood that when God said he would "raise up
your offspring to succeed you," (2 Sam. 7:12) he was talking

about the resurrection of Christ. Again, this is quoting the New Testament Scriptures. Peter is interpreting the Davidic covenant recorded in 2 Samuel 7.

> *Therefore, being a prophet, and knowing that God had sworn with an oath to him that of the fruit of his body, according to the flesh, He would raise up the Christ to sit on his throne, he, foreseeing this, spoke concerning the resurrection of the Christ, that His soul was not left in Hades, nor did His flesh see corruption* (Acts 2:30-32 NKJV).

This covenant was the basis for David's hope in both life and death. He spells this out in 2 Samuel 23:5, his last words.

David rejoices that God made:

> *... an everlasting covenant,*
> *arranged and secured in every part...*
>
> *Will he not bring to fruition my salvation*
> *and grant me my every desire?*

Matthew Henry has some excellent comments on this text.

> God has made a covenant of grace with us in Jesus Christ, and we are here told, *First,* that it is an *everlasting* covenant, from everlasting in the contrivance and counsel of it, and to everlasting in the continuance and consequences of it. *Secondly,* that it is *ordered,* well ordered in all things, admirably well, to advance the glory of God and the honour of the Mediator, together with the holiness and comfort of believers. *Thirdly,* That the promised mercies are sure on the performance of the conditions. *Fourthly,* That it is all our salvation. Nothing but this will save us, and this is sufficient: it is this only upon which our salvation depends. *Fifthly,* That therefore it must be all our desire.[55]

The New Testament immediately announces that Jesus would inherit the Davidic throne and kingdom. When the angel spoke to the Virgin Mary, she was confused. Part of the

---

55 Matthew Henry, *Commentary on the Whole Bible* (Grand Rapids, MI: Zondervan, 1961), 359.

angel's message concerned Jesus receiving the throne of the kingdom promised to his father David.

> *Mary was greatly troubled at his words and wondered what kind of greeting this might be. But the angel said to her, "Do not be afraid, Mary, you have found favor with God. You will be with child and give birth to a son, and you are to give him the name Jesus. He will be great and will be called the Son of the Most High. The Lord God will give him the throne of his father David, and he will reign over the house of Jacob forever; his kingdom will never end"* (Luke 1:29-33).

Acts 2 is a crucial passage. Like most key passages, it is also very controversial. The first section records the coming of the Holy Spirit and the subsequent speaking in tongues. The unbelieving Jews said those speaking in tongues were drunk (vv. 1–13). Peter shows that the event was the fulfillment of two Old Testament prophecies. First, the promise of the Gospel and establishing the kingdom promised in the prophet Joel (vv. 14-21). Second the promise to David (2 Sam. 7) to raise one of his sons from the dead and crown him as king over an eternal kingdom (vv. 22-36).

We will begin by looking at Acts 16-21. Peter says the phenomenon of tongues was an evidence of a prophecy that was made by the prophet Joel is being fulfilled. It is clear that Peter spiritualized Joel's prophecy. Peter definitely understood that the kingdom prophesied in Joel was fulfilled on the day of Pentecost. The gift of the Holy Spirit was the proof that Christ was enthroned in heaven on David's throne and the promised kingdom had come. There is no way you can take Peter's interpretation "literally" without seeing that he spiritualized Joel's prophecy.

> *No, this is what was spoken by the prophet Joel:* ["this is what" cannot mean anything but "this is what."]

> *"'In the last days, God says,*
> *I will pour out my Spirit on all people.*
> *Your sons and daughters will prophesy,*

your young men will see visions,
your old men will dream dreams.

   Even on my servants, both men and women,
I will pour out my Spirit in those days,
and they will prophesy.

   I will show wonders in the heaven above
and signs on the earth below,
blood and fire and billows of smoke.

   The sun will be turned to darkness
and the moon to blood
before the coming of the great and glorious day of the Lord.

   And everyone who calls
on the name of the Lord will be saved.

Dispensationalism cannot spiritualize kingdom promises and must therefore insist the events of Pentecost are only a type or prefiguring of the kingdom promised in Joel. In that system, the words "this is what" which was spoken by Peter must be understood to mean that Pentecost is not a fulfillment of Joel's prophecy but only a prefiguring of what will happen when Christ, in the future, establishes the Davidic (millennial) kingdom. John MacArthur is typical of dispensational writers. Here are two quotations from his Study Bible. The first quotation is from the introduction to the Book of Joel, and the second one is from Acts 2.

   A second issue confronting the interpreter is Peter's quotation from Joel 2:28-32 in Acts 2:16-21. Some have viewed the phenomena of Acts 2 and the destruction of Jerusalem A.D. 70 as the fulfillment of the Joel passage, while others have reserved its fulfillment to the final Day of the Lord only—but clearly Joel is referring to the final terrible Day of the Lord. The pouring out of the Holy Spirit at Pentecost is not a fulfillment, but a preview and sample of the Spirit's power and work, to be released fully and finally in the Messiah's kingdom after the Day of the Lord.[56]

Joel's prophecy will not be completely fulfilled until the millennial kingdom and the final judgment. But Peter by using it, shows that Pentecost was a pre-fulfillment, a taste of what will happen in the millennial kingdom when the Spirit is poured out on all flesh ... [57]

Peter next gives us the new covenant fulfillment of the covenant made with David in 2 Samuel 7. He first shows that Christ had all the credentials to prove that he was David's greater son to whom the kingdom promises had been made.

"Men of Israel, listen to this: Jesus of Nazareth was a man accredited by God to you by miracles, wonders and signs, which God did among you through him, as you yourselves know" (Acts 2:22).

Despite the fact that Jesus gave ample proof that he was David's son who was the heir the Davidic throne and kingdom, the Jews still crucified him, but God raised him from the dead as prophesied in the Davidic covenant.

This man was handed over to you by God's set purpose and foreknowledge; and you, with the help of wicked men, put him to death by nailing him to the cross. But God raised him from the dead, freeing him from the agony of death, because it was impossible for death to keep its hold on him (Acts 2:23, 24).

Peter assures us that David died in the sure hope that not only would he be raised from the dead, but one of his sons would be the Messiah who establish the eternal kingdom promised to David's greater son.

David said about him:

"'I saw the Lord always before me.
Because he is at my right hand,
I will not be shaken.

---

[56] MacArthur, *Study Bible,* 1268.

[57] Ibid., 1635.

Therefore my heart is glad and my tongue rejoices;
my body also will live in hope,

because you will not abandon me to the grave,
nor will you let your Holy One see decay.

You have made known to me the paths of life;
you will fill me with joy in your presence' (Acts 2:25–28).

The next few verses give us the Holy Spirit's interpretation of how David understood the covenant that God made with him.

"Brothers, I can tell you confidently that the patriarch David died and was buried, and his tomb is here to this day" (Acts 2:29).

Why would Peter emphasize that David was dead and buried? Because the covenant to raise up one of his sons and seat him on the throne of an eternal kingdom was to be fulfilled while "you [David] rest with your fathers" (2 Sam. 7:12; cf. 1 Chr. 17:11). The Davidic kingdom was to be established with a resurrected Christ but *before* David was resurrected. David's son would be raised from the dead and the kingdom would be established while David rested with the fathers. He is still sleeping in the grave and will remain there until the second coming. Again, this is not idle speculation. David understood this timing of the establishing of the kingdom. Read the following verses carefully. It is impossible to read a future earthly kingdom into Peter's words. Peter specifically identifies the time of David assuming the kingship of the kingdom was at the resurrection of Christ while David was still in the grave. It is definitely past—not future. It happened when David's greater son was raised from the dead and David was still dead and buried. The whole argument of verses 30-34 hinges on the fact that the resurrection of Christ, not the resurrection of David, established the kingdom promised to David concerning one of his sons. Follow Peter's argument carefully in Acts 2:30-36. Note how clearly Peter shows that the Davidic covenant has been fulfilled and David's greater son is presently seated in heaven on the Davidic throne. There is a not a hint of an earthly future kingdom.

> *But he was a prophet and knew that God had promised him on oath that he would place one of his descendants on his throne. Seeing what was ahead, he spoke of the resurrection of the Christ,* [The Davidic covenant promised that one of David's sons, not David, would be raised from the dead and seated on a throne. The establishing of this throne and kingdom would take place at the resurrection of Christ and not at a supposed future millennium when David will be raised from the dead] *that he was not abandoned to the grave, nor did his body see decay. God has raised this Jesus* [not David] *to life, and we are all witnesses of the fact. Exalted to the right hand of God* [This cannot be referring to David since he is not exalted at the Father's right hand. David has not ascended to heaven], *he has received from the Father the promised Holy Spirit and has poured out what you now see and hear. For David did not ascend to heaven, and yet he said,*

> *"'The Lord said to my Lord:*
> *"Sit at my right hand*

> *until I make your enemies*
> *a footstool for your feet."'*

> *"Therefore let all Israel be assured of this: God has made this Jesus, whom you crucified, both Lord and Christ"* (Acts 2: 30-36).

It is interesting that Peter said that God made Jesus both Lord and Christ. We would expect him to say, "Lord and Savior."

Christ,
Our New Covenant Messiah
Chapter 15

I remember hearing a well-known preacher say, "If you want to learn how to preach the gospel, study the book of Acts. There you have the actual sermons of the apostles themselves." Acts chapter 2 records the coming of the Holy Spirit on the day of Pentecost and the apostles speaking in tongues. The people who witnessed this event were utterly amazed. Some asked what was the meaning of the event, and others wrote it off by saying the apostles were drunk.

When the day of Pentecost came, they were all together in one place. Suddenly a sound like the blowing of a violent wind came from heaven and filled the whole house where they were sitting. They saw what seemed to be tongues of fire that separated and came to rest on each of them. All of them were filled with the Holy Spirit and began to speak in other tongues as the Spirit enabled them.

Now there were staying in Jerusalem God-fearing Jews from every nation under heaven. When they heard this sound, a crowd came together in bewilderment, because each one heard them speaking in his own language. Utterly amazed, they asked: "Are not all these men who are speaking Galileans? Then how is it that each of us hears them in his own native language? Parthians, Medes and Elamites; residents of Mesopotamia, Judea and Cappadocia, Pontus and Asia, Phrygia and Pamphylia, Egypt and the parts of Libya near Cyrene; visitors from Rome (both Jews and converts to Judaism); Cretans and Arabs—we hear them declaring the wonders of God in our own tongues!" Amazed and perplexed, they asked one another, "What does this mean?"

Some, however, made fun of them and said, "They have had too much wine" (Acts 2:1—13).

In verses 14-21, Peter begins to address the people. He assures them the apostles are not drunk. Peter declares the events taking place prove that the kingdom promised in the Old Testament was being fulfilled. He cites two Old Testament passages as being fulfilled at Pentecost. He first declares that the kingdom promised in the book of Joel has come.

> *Then Peter stood up with the Eleven, raised his voice and addressed the crowd: "Fellow Jews and all of you who live in Jerusalem, let me explain this to you; listen carefully to what I say. These men are not drunk, as you suppose. It's only nine in the morning! No, this is what was spoken by the prophet Joel:*
>
> *'In the last days, God says,*
> *I will pour out my Spirit on all people.*
> *Your sons and daughters will prophesy,*
> *your young men will see visions,*
> *your old men will dream dreams.*
>
> *Even on my servants, both men and women,*
> *I will pour out my Spirit in those days,*
> *and they will prophesy.*
>
> *I will show wonders in the heaven above*
> *and signs on the earth below,*
> *blood and fire and billows of smoke.*
>
> *The sun will be turned to darkness*
> *and the moon to blood*
>
> *before the coming of the great and glorious day of the Lord.*
>
> *And everyone who calls*
> *on the name of the Lord will be saved'"* (Acts 2: 14-21).

He then shows that the kingdom and the throne promised to one of David's sons have been established. The kingdom has come, and David's son, Christ the Messiah, is sitting on the throne promised to David.

Jesus had all the credentials to prove he was the promised seed of David, the Messiah. The Jews still crucified him but God raised him from the dead. He ascended to heaven and was given authority over all people (cf. John 17:1-3). Christ is the exalted son of David, the Messiah, who sent the Holy Spirit on the day of Pentecost. The tongues were the evidence of the ascension and exaltation of Christ. Our Lord earned the right, or authority, to send the Spirit as his vicar. Follow Peter's argument carefully in the following verses in Acts 2. First, Jesus had all the credentials to prove his claims that he was the promised Messiah. The Jews still "refused to have this man to rule over us" and crucified him. His Father raised him from the dead, seated him at his own right hand, and gave him a new name, the name "Lord." The new name denoted his earned authority to save or damn all people (cf. John 17:1-3). The great lesson to be learned is set forth in verse 36, "Therefore let all Israel be assured of this: God has made this Jesus, whom you crucified, both Lord and Christ [Messiah (HCSB)]." The heart of the lesson concerns the lordship of Christ. He is the one who fulfills the office of New Covenant King. The very same Jesus that the Jews crucified was raised from the dead and declared by the Father to be Lord over every sinner.

> "Men of Israel, listen to this: Jesus of Nazareth was a man accredited by God to you by miracles, wonders and signs, which God did among you through him, as you yourselves know. This man was handed over to you by God's set purpose and foreknowledge; and you, with the help of wicked men, put him to death by nailing him to the cross. But God raised him from the dead, freeing him from the agony of death, because it was impossible for death to keep its hold on him. David said about him:
>
> 'I saw the Lord always before me.
> Because he is at my right hand,
> I will not be shaken.
>
> Therefore my heart is glad and my tongue rejoices;
> my body also will live in hope,

because you will not abandon me to the grave,
nor will you let your Holy One see decay.

You have made known to me the paths of life;
you will fill me with joy in your presence.'

"Brothers, I can tell you confidently that the patriarch David died and was buried, and his tomb is here to this day. But he was a prophet and knew that God had promised him on oath that he would place one of his descendants on his throne. Seeing what was ahead, he spoke of the resurrection of the Christ, that he was not abandoned to the grave, nor did his body see decay. God has raised this Jesus to life, and we are all witnesses of the fact. Exalted to the right hand of God, he has received from the Father the promised Holy Spirit and has poured out what you now see and hear. For David did not ascend to heaven, and yet he said,

'The Lord said to my Lord:
"Sit at my right hand

until I make your enemies
a footstool for your feet."'

"Therefore let all Israel be assured of this: God has made this Jesus, whom you crucified, both Lord and Christ" (Acts 2:22–36).

Verse 36 is the conclusion to Peter's explanation of the events of Pentecost. It is also the heart of the new covenant gospel, "Therefore let all Israel be assured of this: God has made this Jesus, whom you crucified, both Lord and Christ [Messiah]." In Scripture Jesus is set forth as our "Lord" and "Savior" but in present day preaching it is only "Savior" that is emphasized. The phrase "accept Christ as your personal Savior" is never used in the New Testament. It would be just as correct to say you must "accept Christ as your personal Prophet" or "accept Christ as your personal King." The whole concept of preaching in most churches today can be summed up in that phrase "accept Christ as your personal Savior." The emphasis in Acts is totally different. In Acts the emphasis is on the resurrection and ascension of Christ. The saving benefits of Christ are never separated from his lordship. You may quote Luke 2:11, "today a Savior, who is Messiah the Lord, was born for you in the city of David." (HCSB) and say, "This text says a Savior is born to us." True, but the text also states that this Savior is "Messiah the Lord."

I am not objecting to the word *accept*. I am not suggesting that the phrase *accepting Christ* should be changed to *receiving Christ* even though I prefer using the word *receive*. I remember a dear brother made a big issue out of this. He refused to say, "You must accept the gospel." He felt the word accept means we have a free will. He said that phrase implied the sinner has the ability to both reject and believe the gospel and thus the phrase taught man has a free will. He insisted we should say, "receive Christ." He likened it to pouring water into a bucket. The bucket does not "accept the water," for it is totally passive; the bucket merely "receives the water." Likewise, we do not accept Christ; we receive Christ. I told the man that we are not buckets. We are creatures with a mind, heart, and will, and all three parts of our humanity must be affected by the gospel. The mind must be illuminated by the Holy Spirit, the heart or affections must be penetrated by the truth of the gospel, and the will must be liberated by the same gospel. When biblical regeneration takes place, we gladly accept Christ. When the Holy Spirit gives you a new heart, you will willingly accept Christ.

I once asked my friend, "If I show you a Bible text that says we should 'accept the gospel,' will you change your mind?" When he agreed, I showed him 1 Timothy 1:15, "Here is a trustworthy saying that deserves full acceptance: Christ Jesus came into the world to save sinners—of whom I am the worst." The text says the gospel is worthy of full acceptance, so what is wrong with telling someone to accept it?

If we desire to follow the apostolic preaching of the New Testament, we must preach a whole Christ, meaning we should set forth our Lord as the New Covenant Prophet, Priest, and King. Likewise, we must insist just as much that we preach a gospel which affects every part of man's being, namely his (1) mind, (2) heart and (3) will. The whole man must be affected by the whole Christ. Paul is quite clear in stating this fact in Romans 6:17. I have inserted numbers to highlight the gospel affecting man's whole being. By nature we are slaves of sin, but thanks to God's sovereign electing grace (it is always God's grace and never man's will that is the motivating factor that delivers us). "But thanks be to God that, though you used to be slaves to sin, you (2) wholeheartedly (3) obeyed the (1) form of teaching to which you were entrusted."

First of all, "form of teaching" means the gospel. The gospel first addresses the sinner's mind. As we will see, the gospel must move the heart or affections, but it reaches the heart via the mind. Biblical preaching presents verbal and rational truth. The gospel does not come to us in dreams and visions; it comes to us in clear words. It does not come to us with either water being sprinkled on us or our being totally immersed in water. The gospel does not come to us in communion cups or on a membership card in a local church. That "form of teaching" which is essential to biblical preaching and true salvation always comes to us in propositional form. It states God's Word that must be understood and believed. It also lists man's false ideas that must be rejected. God does not save us in an intellectual vacuum. We are rational beings. God made us that way. He treats us as rational beings. The mind must be instructed with gospel facts before we can be saved.

Second, the biblical facts that must illuminate and penetrate the heart or affections concern the character of an offended God, the nature and reality of sin, and the promises of full and free forgiveness of all sins through the shed blood of Christ. When the Holy Spirit does his regenerating work, the sinner does far more than merely believe some facts, even the right facts. He no longer reads Romans 3:23 and understands in some general sense that all people without exception are sinners. He now feels like God is speaking directly to him. The text now personalized means, "I am the helpless guilty sinner." He feels like God is addressing him directly as an individual. The sinner freely admits that his guilt is dyed deep red and is totally without excuse. He openly acknowledges his lost estate.

The third part of man that must be affected by the Holy Spirit applying the gospel truths is the will. By nature the will is chained to sin and self and must be set free, enabling us to believe the truth. We do not get a second mind, heart, and will. In one sense we repent and believe with the same mind, heart, and will with which we rejected the truth. In another sense, the mind, heart, and will are all "new" in the sense that the Holy Spirit frees them from dominion to sin and self. The action of the will follows the mind and the heart. The will chooses what the heart finds desirable, and the heart finds desirable what the mind finds appealing. We choose to do what pleases us. Before our mind is regenerated by the Holy Spirit, we can only desire to please ourselves. The sinful mind (or nature) hates God and his truth (cf. Rom. 8:7). When the Holy Spirit regenerates the mind and heart, we find trusting Christ to be most desirable.

We cannot even *want* to be saved until the gospel illuminates our mind to see the real beauty of Christ, but when the Holy Spirit does his regenerating work, we cannot not want to believe. We are given a new mind only in the sense that our natural mind is retaught by the gospel truths enabling us to believe the gospel. Paul calls this work of sovereign grace the "obedience of faith" (Rom. 16:26 KJV).

It is obvious that God's goal in the redeeming work of Christ is having a gospel that brings sinners into submission to Christ as both Lord and Savior, "Now to him who is able to establish you by my gospel and the proclamation of Jesus Christ, according to the revelation of the mystery hidden for long ages past, but now revealed and made known through the prophetic writings by the command of the eternal God, so that all nations might believe and *obey him*" (italics added) (Rom. 16:25-27). Or we could say, following Luke 2:11, to bow to a savior who is Lord.

Imagine for a moment that a lost person says, "I want to be a true Christian. I want to be a true follower of Christ. I sincerely believe that Christ is the true and final Prophet of God. I am going to obey his teaching because I believe that he alone speaks for God. I will gladly submit to his authority as my King. However, I do not believe in the idea of the need for a blood sacrifice to pay for my sins. I believe the whole system of blood sacrifice is pagan in origin." We would have to say to such an individual, "I am sorry but you cannot become a Christian with such a belief. Christ as Prophet, Priest, and King is a package deal."

There are many people who will extol wonderful things about Jesus as the greatest teacher that ever lived but will balk at the doctrine of propitiation. Actually, the word *propitiation* is probably one of the most hated words in the Bible.

Suppose another person says, "I thank God for the cross and atoning blood of Christ. I believe the shed blood of Christ is my only hope of salvation. However, I do not think Christ was correct in everything he taught. He was a man of his times. Some of his views are not consistent with what we have come to believe today." Again we would have to say, "I am sorry but you cannot become a Christian on those terms. You cannot have Christ as your priest to pay for your sins and then reject him as your prophet. It is a package deal." The current view that teaches you can receive Christ as your Savior but, at the same time, reject him as Lord over your life is not at all the gospel of the New Testament. If we desire that sinners see the face of God in peace, we must proclaim the whole Christ—Prophet, Priest, and King—to the whole man—mind, heart, and will.

The modern day gospel misunderstands at least two major points concerning our subject. One, it reduces saving faith to being only an activity of the mind. Gospel faith is not merely believing some facts are true. It is receiving a person and trusting him to fulfill a promise he made. When someone says, "I believe in Christ," I ask them, "What do you believe in him for? What do you trust him to do?" A forgiven sinner has some knowledge of forgiveness by the blood shedding on the cross. Believing in Christ as our Lord and Savior is not the same as "believing Columbus crossed the ocean blue in 1492." Anyone can believe that fact, or any other historical fact is true, but no one can "believe in Christ" in the biblical sense apart from God's sovereign electing grace.

Two, when we receive Christ, we do not receive facts; we receive a person, and that person is the Lord of glory himself. We receive Christ in a way that is not true in any other relationship between two people. Paul said, "I know a man *in* (italics added) Christ ..." (2 Cor. 12:2). The Bible is the only literature ever written at any time in history, in any language, or in any style that describes a relationship of two people as one person being "in" the other person. Every believer is baptized into Christ. That is unique language because it is an unique experience. Scripture speaks of our being in Christ and Christ being in us. This descriptive language is unique to the Word of God.

The apostle John introduces his gospel by asserting the absolute deity of Christ. He was the creator of the world. He came into the world he created. He came unto his own, and they rejected him. But some received him. Notice it was a person they received, "all who received him, to those who believed in his name," (John 1:12). Salvation is being joined to that person by a living faith. Of course, those who received Christ believed the essential facts about him, but the facts pointed to a person. Salvation is not in the facts but in the person to whom the facts pointed.

Technically speaking, we believe the testimony of the Father concerning his perfect satisfaction with the work of atonement accomplished by Christ. The work of atonement, made by Christ on the cross, was directed toward the Father. Christ's obedient life and death fulfilled the work of atonement that Christ accomplished as our substitute. This work was directed to the Father. Christ "offered himself unblemished to God," (Heb. 9:14). The atoning work of blood shedding was essential to satisfy God's holy character. The resurrection, ascension, seating at the Father's right hand, and receiving full authority to forgive whom he chose was all involved in Christ being given the new name of "Lord" as a reward for his atoning work. Verse 37 in Acts 2 records the response of the unbelieving Jews to Peter's explanation of the events of Pentecost.

> *When the people heard this, they were cut to the heart and said to Peter and the other apostles, "Brothers, what shall we do?"*

Verses 38-39 are surely on any list of most misused texts of Scripture. Verse 38 is used as a proof text to prove that you must be baptized in order to be saved. If this is the meaning, then we must rewrite many texts that make it very clear that baptism is not essential to salvation.

> Peter replied, "Repent and be baptized, every one of you, in the name of Jesus Christ for the forgiveness of your sins. And you will receive the gift of the Holy Spirit" (Acts 2:38).

Verse 39 is a key text used by those who believe in infant baptism. I have been a student of the Word of God for over fifty years. I have been in many discussions by mail and face to face. I have been forced to revise my understanding on more than one occasion. I have seen good and godly men twist Scripture verses at the expense of clear truth in order to hang onto a creed. I must say that using Acts 2:39 as a proof text for infant baptism is simply astounding. It denies and defies every rule of biblical exegesis. It is one of the most glaring examples of bad interpretation that I know.

> "The promise is for you and your children and for all who are far off—for all whom the Lord our God will call" (Acts 2:39).

The paedobaptist view of Acts 2:39 is clearly set forth by Robert Shaw in his widely used exposition of the *Westminster Confession of Faith*. The "promise" in Acts 2:39 is said to be the covenant of grace made with Abraham. That same promise is said to be made with Christian parents and their children. For a moment, assume that is correct. Assume further that Shaw is correct, and then we must read Acts 2:39 this way, "The promise of the covenant made with Abraham is the same promise made to the people to whom Peter spoke on the day of Pentecost." There is not a single shred of evidence for reading that into the verse. You must ignore what the text actually says and read into the text what is not there.

I am reminded of the story of Spurgeon and the Anglican priest. The Anglican priest wanted to discuss infant baptism. He said to Spurgeon, "I will read a verse of Scripture in favor of infant baptism and in response you give a verse for your view." The Anglican quoted Matthew 19:14: "Let the little children come to me ..." Spurgeon thought a moment and then quoted Job 1:1, "In the land of Uz there lived a man whose name was Job." The Anglican asked, "What in the world does that verse have to do with infant baptism?" Spurgeon replied, "The same as Matthew 19:14, nothing at all." Acts 2:39 has absolutely nothing to do with infant baptism. Here is Robert Shaw's comment:

> We thus find, that when God established his covenant with Abraham, he embraced his infant seed in that covenant; and that the promise made to Abraham and to his seed is still endorsed to us is evident from the express declaration of the Apostle Peter (Acts ii:39): "The promise is unto you, and to your children." If children are included in the covenant, we conclude that they have a right to baptism, the seal of the covenant. [58]

The first thing Shaw has to find in the text in order to use it as a proof text is evidence that Peter is speaking to believing parents. The "you" being promised has to be proven to be believers concerning their children sharing in the "promise" made to Abraham. The problem is that *Peter is addressing lost sinners! He is not speaking to believing parents.* The promise being mentioned is clearly spelled out in verse 21. It is "everyone who calls on the name of the Lord will be saved." Peter is preaching the gospel to the very people who literally crucified the Son of God. The "promise" is given in response to the question asked by the lost Jews with the blood of Christ on their hands. They asked, "What shall we do?"

> *Peter replied, "Repent and be baptized, every one of you, in the name of Jesus Christ for the forgiveness of your sins"* (Acts 2:38).

This verse has nothing to do with believing parents. It has to do with ungodly sinners who crucified Christ. You don't

---

[58] Robert Shaw, *The Reformed Faith, An Exposition of the Westminster Confession of Faith* (Scotland, UK: Christian Focus Publications, 2008), 366.

instruct *believing parents* to "save yourselves from this corrupt generation" (Acts 2:40b).

The second thing Shaw needs to explain is how non-covenant children (those children not born in a Christian home) are included in the "promise." Notice carefully exactly what Acts 2:39 says. It is Peter's response to the question asked in verse 37 by the convicted but still lost Jews who crucified Christ. It was the promise of salvation to all who call on the Lord in saving faith. This same promise is made to the children of the ungodly Jews if they will believe this same "whosoever shall" (cf. Acts 2:21) gospel. This very same promise is made to these lost Jews, and is made to their children, and is also made to "all who are far off." That would be the Gentiles. In other words, the pagans have the identical same promise of the gospel as do the lost Jews and their children. If the promise means the covenant of grace, then the pagans are just as included in it as are the lost Jews and their children.

There is one more difficulty for those who want to get the infants of believing parents into Acts 2:39. That which governs who believes the promise in Acts 2:39 is not physical birth but sovereign election. Peter is quite clear that all the elect will realize the promise. Salvation is not determined by your birth certificate and who your parents are; the new birth experience is determined by sovereign electing grace—*even as many as the Lord our God shall call.* The phrase, "…for all whom the Lord our God will call" governs the whole verse. In other words, the promise will be realized by 1) as many of those who are effectually called from among those who heard Peter preach on the day of Pentecost, 2) as many of the children who are effectually called, and 3) as many from among the pagans who will be called.

There is not a single word about a special promise to the children of believers in this text. The children of believers have no more promised to them than do the Gentile pagans who are far off. What is clear is that some children of believing parents are among the elect and some are not. The Lord who is both the only Savior and the only judge saves whom he will. The promise of salvation is to all who believe the gospel. All of these are synonymous with all those who are elect regardless of whether they are among the Jews or the Gentiles. The one doing the choosing in every case is God. If you chose to believe in infant baptism—God bless you—but please, do not use Acts 2:39 as a proof text. If you claim to believe and preach a biblical gospel, make sure it begins and ends with Jesus Christ as Lord of Lord and King of Kings.

Scripture Index